Self Help for Billionaires

SHIPA TABS 1

Also from EATMS Productions

Books on power, survival, women's autonomy, and the systems shaping modern America.

Nonfiction

Billionaires, Capitalism, and Power

Evil and the Mountain Ungreed
Self Help for American Billionaires
Selfish Steve and the Ivory Tower
Tariffs, Taxes, & Face-Eating Leopards
Ban Billionaires: Fascism Fix

Fascism, Religion, and Cultural Control

Self Help for the Manosphere
Fascism 2025
Fascism & the Perverts & the Greed Virus
Christian Fascism Marriage Book
Tyranny, Table Manners, & Tiramisu

Guides for Women's Autonomy and Protection

How to Survive in Post-America as a Woman
Project 2025 American Drag
4B – Burn, Ban, Boycott, Build
4B OG – So No Go GYN
I'm Glad He's Dead

Analysis of Authoritarian Project 2025

Project 2025: The Blueprint
Project 2025: The List
Project 2025, Christian Dumb Dumbs, & The Republican Agenda
Fascism, Project 2025, & The Pinkprint

Modern Rewrites for Women

Stoic Principles Reimagined
Siddhartha Reimagined
The Prince Reimagined for Women
The Art of War Reimagined for Women
The Jungle Reimagined
The Constitution Reimagined for Women

Machine Learning Series

AI, Bitcoin, Nostr for Women
AI, Safety, & Security for Women
AI, Anxiety, & Health for Women
AI, Kids, & Family Safety for Women
AI, Creativity, & Personal Expression for Women
AI, Independent Work, & Parallel Power for Women

Social Systems Series

Emotional Labor for Women
Household Power for Women
Workplace Power for Women
Medical Bias for Women
Aging Systems for Women
Recovery Systems for Women

Fiction

Dystopian Stories of Resistance and Collapse

Propaganda Paige & the Missing Prosperity
Propaganda Paige & the TIDE Manifesto
Propaganda Paige & the Shadow Cartographers
Propaganda Paige & the Prosperity Alliance
Propaganda Paige & the Shattered Truth
Propaganda Paige & the Rising TIDE
Propaganda Paige & the Last Bastion
Propaganda Paige & the Dawn of Prosperity
Project 2025: Dorian — The Last Men
Project 2025: Boy — A Last Men Novel

Self Help For Billionaires

Self Help is Performative Acquiescence To a Broken System
(SHIPA TABS) 1

A PARODY

by
Esme Mees

EATMS
PRODUCTIONS

Self Help For Billionaires

Self Help is Performative Acquiescence To a Broken System
(SHIPA TABS) 1

A PARODY

by
Esme Mees

EATMS
PRODUCTIONS

Modern Rewrites for Women

Stoic Principles Reimagined
Siddhartha Reimagined
The Prince Reimagined for Women
The Art of War Reimagined for Women
The Jungle Reimagined
The Constitution Reimagined for Women

Machine Learning Series

AI, Bitcoin, Nostr for Women
AI, Safety, & Security for Women
AI, Anxiety, & Health for Women
AI, Kids, & Family Safety for Women
AI, Creativity, & Personal Expression for Women
AI, Independent Work, & Parallel Power for Women

Social Systems Series

Emotional Labor for Women
Household Power for Women
Workplace Power for Women
Medical Bias for Women
Aging Systems for Women
Recovery Systems for Women

Fiction

Dystopian Stories of Resistance and Collapse

Propaganda Paige & the Missing Prosperity
Propaganda Paige & the TIDE Manifesto
Propaganda Paige & the Shadow Cartographers
Propaganda Paige & the Prosperity Alliance
Propaganda Paige & the Shattered Truth
Propaganda Paige & the Rising TIDE
Propaganda Paige & the Last Bastion
Propaganda Paige & the Dawn of Prosperity
Project 2025: Dorian — The Last Men
Project 2025: Boy — A Last Men Novel

Copyright © 2024 Eatms Productions
All rights reserved.

No part of this book may be reproduced, or stored in a retrieval system, or transmitted in any form or by any means, electronic, mechanical, photocopying, recording, or otherwise, without express permission in writing from the publisher.

This book is a work of opinion and creative interpretation. While some names and events may be referenced or alluded to, any claims made are based on publicly available information and are intended as satire, parody, or commentary on societal and political issues. The content should not be interpreted as factual assertions about any individual or entity. The author does not intend to defraud, defame, or mislead, and encourages readers to form their own conclusions. Any resemblance to real persons, living or dead, is purely coincidental unless explicitly noted otherwise.

ISBN: 978-1-966014-04-1

Cover, interior design, interior prints by: Esme Mees

eatms@pm.me
www.eatms.me

Printed in the United States of America.

Greed has driven the world crazy.

- Nina Simone

Table of Contents

Introduction: Congratulations You Filthy Parasite	9
Chapter 1: Affirmations of the Ruthless	15
Chapter 2: The Art of Hoarding	33
Chapter 3: Faking Philanthropy	43
Chapter 4: Networking on Super Yachts	51
Chapter 5: Billionaire Burnout	59
Chapter 6: How to Handle Bad Press	67
Chapter 7: Offloading Responsibility	79
Chapter 8: Identifying with the Working Class	95
Chapter 9: Love in the Time of Power	113
Chapter 10: Creating Legacy without Effort	125
Chapter 11: Embracing Your Inner Supervillain	137
Chapter 12: Preparing for the Revolution	151
Epilogue: Greed is an Illness, I am Ill	163
Appendices	167
List of Prints	171
About the author	173

Introduction
Congratulations You Filthy Parasite!

Welcome to the Club of Gods and Gargoyles

Congratulations, you've done it. You've ascended to the highest tier of human achievement: amassing so much wealth that the normal rules of decency, physics, and accountability no longer apply to you. You're not just rich, you're untouchable. You can buy politicians like others buy groceries, hoard more property than entire neighborhoods, and accumulate private jets as if they were keychains. But don't mistake yourself for a god; no one's here to worship. You're more like a gargoyle, perched high above the crumbling cathedral of late-stage capitalism, stone-faced, immovable, and oblivious to the rot festering below. From up there, it probably looks like everything is under control. People scraping by on minimum wage might appear like ants, scurrying around, their struggles too tiny to notice. Meanwhile, you float through life insulated by designer suits, exclusive events, and private islands, surrounded by a chorus of sycophants who convince you that your net worth reflects your moral worth. But deep down, you know that without the labyrinth of offshore accounts, shell companies, and exploited labor holding you up, you'd come crashing down like a marble statue shattered on impact.

The truth is, the rest of us aren't mesmerized by your wealth, we're exhausted by it. We aren't applauding from the sidelines as you buy a new yacht; we're standing in line at food banks, trying to survive in a world that has been rigged in your favor. In a just society, your endless accumulation of wealth would be seen not as success but as pathology, a glaring sign of a system so morally bankrupt that it celebrates hoarding while children go to bed hungry. But hey, it's not your fault, right? The system was designed by people like you, for people like you. And why would you change a game you've already won? So sit back, relax, and enjoy this satirical self-help guide, because if the world is going to burn, at least you can toast marshmallows from the deck of your superyacht. After all, being a billionaire means never having to care, never apologizing, and never worrying about the mess left behind for the rest of us to clean up. Welcome to the club, gargoyle, your perch is ready.

Why Feel Sorry for Yourself When You Can Buy Feelings?

Being a billionaire seems so exhausting, doesn't it? All those hedge funds to monitor, boardrooms to dominate, and personal chefs to keep happy. And let's not forget the hardest part: convincing the rest of the world that your wealth is some kind of burden. Cue the violins. We've all heard it before, how lonely it is at the top, how no one understands the immense responsibility of owning twelve vacation homes, and how exhausting it is to buy every politician with just the right amount of plausible deniability. But let's cut through the nonsense, shall we? No one's shedding a tear for your existential crisis, and no amount of beachfront property will make it seem like you've got it worse than the single mother working three jobs just to keep her kids fed.

Here's the dirty little secret: your wealth didn't just happen because you worked harder or dreamed bigger than everyone else. It's a carefully choreographed performance, built on exploitation, systemic inequality, and some conveniently lax tax laws. Yet somehow, billionaires have convinced the rest of us to feel bad for them. As if flying first-class on the struggle bus is even remotely relatable. But let's be honest, if money doesn't buy happiness, you haven't spent enough of it trying. Feeling unfulfilled? No problem. Just buy some meaning. There are life coaches, private therapists, and motivational retreats all designed to assure you that the problem isn't your obscene wealth; it's that you just haven't *centered your energy* properly. Burn some sage on that yacht. Cleanse your chakras in a $40,000 wellness bath. That hollow feeling will pass, probably around the time you purchase another startup to crush.

The real kicker, though, is how you still manage to frame your success as a burden, an unlucky side effect of being *too visionary*. As if the millions of people struggling to survive wouldn't trade places with you in a heartbeat, just to catch their breath. But don't worry, this book isn't here to nag or guilt-trip you about your greed. We're here to poke fun, and maybe, just maybe, help the rest of the world see how ridiculous it is that we allow people to hoard such staggering wealth while others sleep on the streets. So go ahead, billionaire. Keep chasing that elusive happiness. Just remember: the rest of us are too busy scraping by to feel sorry for you.

Extreme Wealth Isn't a Goal—It's a Diagnosis

Let's get something straight: becoming a billionaire isn't a sign of brilliance, it's a symptom of a profoundly sick system. You didn't win life's meritocracy lottery; you hacked it. Extreme wealth is what happens when ambition goes untreated, metastasizing into a full-blown obsession with accumulation. Somewhere along the way, society confused "success" with "hoarding." But make no mistake: billionaires aren't inspirational, they're case studies in unchecked greed. Your wealth isn't proof of innovation; it's the corporate equivalent of binge eating while millions starve. There's no elegant way to sugarcoat the truth: when you have more money than you could possibly spend in a hundred lifetimes, that's not just excess, t's theft, plain and simple.

And what's worse is that this behavior has become so normalized that people don't even blink when the ultra-rich claim they deserve it all. We've been brainwashed into thinking that building obscene wealth is the pinnacle of human achievement, even as the pillars holding up society, healthcare, education, housing, crumble beneath us. But let's be honest: if your success relies on squeezing wages, dodging taxes, and lobbying politicians to keep loopholes intact, then you aren't a genius. You're just a well-dressed parasite with a PR team. The idea that billionaires are somehow benevolent leaders guiding humanity toward a brighter future is a fantasy, like expecting a vampire to donate blood.

In a functional society, no one would be allowed to hoard such wealth while others suffer. We'd call it what it really is: an economic disorder. You can slap a fancy title on it, "entrepreneur," "visionary," "philanthropist," but deep down, it's hoarding with a logo. A reasonable society would see billionaires not as icons to be admired but as emergencies to be addressed, much like an oil spill or a contagious outbreak. If our culture were sane, we wouldn't ask how you got so rich; we'd ask why we ever allowed it to happen in the first place. But here we are, drowning in inequality, patting billionaires on the back for their brilliance while ignoring the rot beneath their fortunes. So yes, billionaire, you may feel like the hero of your own story, but the rest of us see the truth: you're not a savior, you're a symptom.

The Rot Beneath the Gold-Plated Surface

Let's peel back the luxury veneer, shall we? Behind the designer suits, the superyachts, and the influencer-packed birthday parties lies the real story: rot. Not the kind you can cover with marble countertops and bespoke furniture, but the deep moral decay that comes from a society so broken that it rewards greed with worship. Billionaires aren't the solution to the world's problems, they *are* the problem. A world where a handful of people hoard unimaginable wealth while millions starve isn't a quirk of fate; it's the predictable outcome of a rigged system. Extreme wealth isn't just unethical, it's obscene. Your stock buybacks, market manipulation, and tax avoidance schemes aren't genius maneuvers; they're just the playground tricks of people who've never been told "no." We live in a society where hoarding billions is called "ambition," but organizing for fair wages is treated like an act of rebellion. That's not the natural order, that's rot.

And what's most baffling is how society applauds this nonsense. We throw ticker-tape parades for people who earn more in a day than most families see in a lifetime. We hand them medals for "giving back" when all they're doing is tossing pocket change from atop their ivory towers. But let's get real: charity isn't justice. Buying mosquito nets for impoverished countries doesn't absolve you from the fact that your wealth depends on the exploitation of workers all over the globe. And donating to museums in exchange for your name on a wing doesn't make you a philanthropist, it makes you a marketing strategist. This entire charade of benevolence is just another way to distract us from the truth: billionaires exist because the rest of us don't have what we need. If the world made any sense, we'd treat billionaires like toxic spills, contain the damage, clean it up, and make sure it never happens again. But instead, we slap them on the back and let them keep the loot. Here's the deal: we don't need nicer billionaires or more charitable billionaires, we need *fewer billionaires*, period. Because the longer we let a handful of people hold the world hostage with their wealth, the deeper the rot spreads. And no amount of charitable giving, climate summits on yachts, or TED Talks about "changing the world" can disguise that fact.

Ban Billionaires Until Everyone Eats

Here's a radical idea: how about we don't let anyone hoard billions until every human being has a full belly and a safe place to sleep? Sound extreme? Only if you think it's reasonable to let a tiny group of people own more wealth than entire countries while others scrape by on pennies. Billionaires are not the inevitable outcome of hard work and brilliance, they're a side effect of an economic system built on exploitation, wage theft, and inequality. It's not that society can't feed the hungry or house the homeless; it's that we *won't*, because protecting the obscene wealth of the few is somehow more important than ensuring the dignity of the many. Every billion dollars tucked away in an offshore account is food stolen from a child's plate, a roof taken from someone's head, and medicine denied to the sick. And still, the world tiptoes around billionaires, as if criticizing their wealth is the real crime, not the poverty they perpetuate.

But enough with the polite outrage, let's call this what it is. Billionaires are economic arsonists who burn down opportunity for everyone else, and no amount of charitable donations will extinguish the flames. They throw crumbs at social issues while pocketing entire loaves. Their wealth is not a reward for brilliance but a theft from the commons, resources, labor, and potential that could have been used to build a fairer world. If we want to see real change, we need to stop treating billionaires like quirky characters in some absurd rags-to-riches fairy tale and start recognizing them for what they are: obstacles to human progress. So no, we don't need to wait for them to have a change of heart, and we certainly don't need another vanity charity. What we need is a system that bans billionaires altogether, at least until every single person on this planet has the basics: food, housing, healthcare, and dignity.

Because the truth is, there's no version of a just society that allows someone to hoard enough money to buy a fleet of yachts while others go to bed hungry. Billionaires aren't heroes, they're symptoms of a failing system, and the sooner we treat them as such, the better off we'll be. So, consider this little guide a first step, a satirical smack on the wrist to remind everyone that the goal isn't to make nicer billionaires; it's to make *fewer* of them. When everyone has enough, and billionaires are a relic of the past, that's when we're on the right a VIP lounge.

Chapter 1
Affirmations of the Ruthless

Welcome to the Power of Daily Affirmations

There's a certain magic in standing before a mirror and telling yourself exactly what you want to hear, especially when no one around you is willing to argue (or, more accurately, *allowed* to argue). Affirmations aren't just a tool for new-age wellness junkies, they're essential for billionaires like you. After all, the world may see your wealth as obscene, but in your reflection, it looks just right. You've crushed competitors, exploited loopholes, and converted human misery into quarterly profits. And yet, people *still* complain. They accuse you of hoarding resources and dodging taxes, as if ambition and greed weren't two sides of the same shiny coin. That's where affirmations come in. If you repeat something often enough, like "I deserve everything I have, and then some," it becomes true. Reality is just a negotiation, and your bank balance does all the talking.

Affirmations are your mental shield, blocking out the pesky voices of activists, regulators, and workers demanding "fairness," whatever that means. With a carefully curated set of mantras, you can remind yourself that the rules are for other people, empathy is a PR tool, and everything, markets, politics, even people, bends to your will. So yes, affirmations aren't just feel-good nonsense. They're a psychological weapon, a mantra-powered bulldozer designed to pave the way for more acquisitions, more influence, and even more wealth. If the masses are going to vilify you anyway, you might as well feel fantastic about it. Welcome to the art of ruthless affirmation, where the only thing better than being right is believing you're always right. So, gaze into that mirror, adjust your posture, and tell yourself: "I am the economy." Because you are, and if they haven't realized it yet, they'll figure it out soon enough.

Morning Mirror Ritual - Own the Day Before It Owns You

Every billionaire knows that winning the day starts the moment you wake up, preferably in silk sheets with a view of the ocean, a skyline, or a golf course you own. But before diving into your itinerary (which hopefully includes crushing some underdog startups and lobbying against wealth taxes), it's important to center yourself. That's where the morning mirror ritual comes in. You'll need a reflective surface, perhaps the $30,000 custom mirror framed with reclaimed wood from a remote island no one can afford to visit, and at least five uninterrupted minutes. Stare directly into your reflection. This is not vanity. It's *vision alignment*. You aren't just looking at yourself; you're looking at power incarnate. Repeat the following affirmations out loud, with the confidence of someone who could buy and sell their neighbors without batting an eyelash:

1. *"I am inevitable."*
2. *"The market thrives because I say it does."*
3. *"The poor are not my problem, they're my audience."*
4. *"Today is mine, and everything in it will be, too."*

Hold the gaze. Breathe deeply. Ignore the assistant knocking at your door with your organic oat milk latte, this moment is sacred. Feel your posture straighten and your jaw set, because confidence is currency, and you can't spend what you don't have. Let the affirmations soak into your bones. These are your battle hymns, the verbal armor that will protect you from pesky obstacles like regulations, protests, and ethics. If you tell yourself you deserve the world long enough, the universe has no choice but to hand it over on a silver platter.

As a finishing touch, add one final mantra: *"Laws are merely suggestions."* This subtle but crucial reminder will ensure you navigate the day with the right attitude. Rules exist only for those who lack the imagination, or the resources, to rewrite them. Take a deep breath. Roll your shoulders back. Smile just enough to remind yourself that empathy is for the unprofitable. You've centered your energy, reinforced your purpose, and reminded yourself that today belongs to you. Now go out there and own it.

Classic Billionaire Affirmations to Repeat Throughout the Day

It's not enough to start your morning with affirmations, oh no. Billionaires need a steady drip of self-reinforcement, just like they need constant asset growth. Your power isn't something you can just check in with once a day; it requires ongoing maintenance, the way a luxury yacht needs polishing or a media empire needs spin. The key is to seamlessly weave affirmations into your routine. Whether you're lounging on a private jet or slashing payrolls to "increase efficiency," there's always room for a little self-empowerment. Below is a curated selection of billionaire-approved mantras, tailored to keep your head high and your conscience low no matter what the day throws at you:

General Use:
"I am the economy."
(Say this while casually checking stock prices. It works best if you really believe that any dip in your net worth could trigger a recession.)
"Everyone envies me, even if they don't know it yet."
(This one's perfect for board meetings. Maintain eye contact and let your silent superiority speak louder than words.)

After Public Criticism:
"Regulation is for the unimaginative."
(Recite this any time a politician dares to suggest taxing your offshore accounts.)
"If they're mad, I must be doing something right."
(Use this when Twitter explodes over your latest acquisition, policy change, or outlandish take.)

And here's a pro tip: You don't even need to say these affirmations aloud. Just thinking them during meetings or interviews will give you the subtle glow of untouchable self-assurance. It's like manifesting but with fewer crystals and more spreadsheets.

Powerful Situational Affirmations for Specific Moments

Before a Hostile Takeover:
"Monopoly is just a word for being really good at business."
(This one helps remind you that dominance isn't just an option, it's an obligation.)
"If I don't crush them, someone else will."
(This pairs nicely with a smug grin.)

After a Scandal Breaks:
"The narrative is mine to control."
(Ideal for press briefings. Bonus points if you own part of the media reporting on the scandal.)
"Public outrage fades, my fortune doesn't."
(Repeat this whenever someone suggests a PR apology.)

Keep these affirmations in rotation, deploying them as needed. A few well-timed words can turn any challenge into just another step on your golden staircase to even more wealth. Say them often. Say them with conviction. And above all, believe them, because if you believe you deserve everything, the world will fall in line. Or at least, it will once you buy it.

Before Announcing Mass Layoffs:
"Efficiency isn't cruelty, it's strategy."
(Say this as you prepare to cut thousands of jobs while watching your stock price soar.)
"Their sacrifice, my gain."
(Use this to remind yourself that every 'difficult decision' is just part of staying ahead in the game.)
"The market rewards boldness, not sympathy."
(Perfect for silencing any last-minute doubts. Compassion is for HR, profit is for you.)

Power Pose + Affirmation Combos

Power isn't just about what you say, it's about how you carry yourself. Billionaires aren't just rich; they *look* rich, with every movement radiating control, confidence, and the kind of arrogance that says, "I own this room, and maybe the building, too." That's where power posing comes in. Sure, it sounds silly, standing like a comic book hero for two minutes, but research shows it can actually trick your brain into believing you deserve even more than you already have. And if there's anything you're good at, it's believing you're entitled to everything. Pair these power poses with affirmations to supercharge your confidence and ensure your dominance remains unquestioned.

Pose #1: The Master of the Universe (Hands on Hips, Feet Apart)

Stand tall, feet shoulder-width apart, hands on your hips like you just conquered the world (which, let's be honest, you probably did). Tilt your chin up slightly, not too much, just enough to suggest you're evaluating the worthiness of everything around you. While holding this pose, repeat:

- *"I deserve everything I want, and what I want is everything."*
- *"The market obeys me, not the other way around."*

This is the perfect pose for mentally preparing before an earnings call or investor meeting. If you're not convinced of your dominance by the end of two minutes, increase the duration, confidence can't be rushed.

Pose #2: The Thought Leader (Arms Crossed, Slight Lean Back)

Adopt the "I'm too smart for this conversation" stance: cross your arms and lean back slightly, as if you've just heard the dumbest suggestion imaginable. Now, soften your expression to a condescending smile, just enough to communicate, "Bless your heart for trying." While holding this pose, repeat:

- *"Collaboration is optional; control is not."*
- *"I don't need allies, just followers."*

This combo works wonders before any "collaborative" discussion, such as merging companies or negotiating with governments. Remember, you're not looking for agreement, you're waiting for everyone to realize you've already won.

Pose #3: The Relaxed Predator (One Hand in Pocket, Casual Stance)

This pose is for informal dominance, ideal for cocktail parties, yacht gatherings, or post-layoff celebrations. Stand with one hand in your pocket, the other holding a drink. Keep your shoulders relaxed and your gaze steady. While holding this pose, repeat:

- *"Laws are flexible, like people."*
- *"It's not about doing the right thing; it's about doing the profitable thing."*

This stance tells the world you're a shark who doesn't need to bare its teeth—you've already eaten the competition. The key is subtlety; your power should feel effortless, like an ocean tide swallowing a shoreline.

By mastering these poses and affirmations, you'll radiate an aura of control no matter the setting. Power isn't just in wealth—it's in every glance, every gesture, and every pose that tells the world: *I already own you.* And with these combinations in your arsenal, you'll make sure no one ever forgets it.

Pose #4: The Benevolent Overlord (Both Hands Open, Palms Up)

Perfect for charity events and press conferences, this pose screams "generosity" while quietly reinforcing control. Stand with feet grounded, arms extended slightly, palms up, as if offering humanity a gift. Tilt your head just enough to seem attentive without implying anyone's opinion matters. While holding the pose, repeat:

- *"Giving is branding."*
- *"They don't need to thank me, but they will."*
- *"I help because I can, not because I should."*

This stance is ideal for deflecting criticism by presenting yourself as a savior. Use it sparingly, too much fake benevolence could give people the wrong idea that you're starting to care. The goal isn't to change the world, it's to remind everyone they should be grateful you exist.

Affirming Away Guilt - The Magic of Denial

Let's face it, guilt is the enemy of ambition. If every decision came with moral baggage, you'd never get anything done, let alone build an empire. That's why billionaires like you need a special set of affirmations, designed not just to boost your confidence but to banish guilt entirely. Feeling bad is for those who can't afford therapists or PR teams. Your job isn't to question whether your actions are "right" or "fair." Your job is to stay focused on the bottom line, no matter how many people get crushed under it. Guilt is just wasted energy, energy that could be better spent optimizing profits, evading taxes, or lobbying for fewer regulations. The trick is to deny, reframe, and move forward without ever looking back. Here are go-to affirmations for those pesky moments when conscience tries to creep in:

Affirmation #1: *"If my employees wanted higher wages, they'd work harder."*
(This one works best right after approving layoffs or cutting health benefits. Efficiency is key, if they can't survive on what you pay, that's a motivation problem, not yours.)

Affirmation #2: *"Philanthropy is my gift to humanity, whether they deserve it or not."*
(Perfect for press conferences and charity dinners. Remember, it's not about helping, it's about being *seen* helping. If they slap your name on a hospital, even better.)

Affirmation #3: *"Guilt is just another form of weakness, and I don't do weak."*
(This is ideal after finalizing a tax avoidance scheme. Laws are written to be bent, and paying taxes is for the uninspired.)

The key is to reframe any act that might seem exploitative as a necessary business strategy. Layoffs aren't heartless; they're a restructuring. Dodging taxes isn't unethical; it's savvy. Philanthropy? A branding tool with a nice tax deduction attached. Guilt has no place in this world, especially not yours. It's for those who don't know how to leverage power, and if they're upset, it's just proof that they're not playing the game right. Denial isn't just a coping mechanism, it's how you stay focused. After all, if you stop to feel bad, someone else might grab what's rightfully yours. So, repeat these affirmations until they're second nature. With enough practice, guilt will feel like just another inefficiency you can't afford to keep around.

Pre-Meeting Affirmations for Corporate Domination

Meetings may seem like tedious formalities to some, but for you, they're battlegrounds. Every handshake is a power play, every agenda item an opportunity to crush the competition, and every glance a subtle negotiation. Whether it's a quarterly earnings call or a merger discussion, walking into a meeting unprepared is simply not an option. That's where these affirmations come in, think of them as your personal armor. Repeat them on the way to the boardroom, in the back of your limo, or right before you dial into a video call from your villa in Monaco. With these mantras, you won't just attend meetings, you'll dominate them.

Affirmation #1: *"If I don't crush them, someone else will."*
(Use this when sitting across from a rival CEO. Business isn't a friendly game of golf, it's warfare. Either you're the predator, or you're dinner. There's no in-between.)
Affirmation #2: *"Monopoly isn't a dirty word, it's the dream."*
(Ideal for merger talks. A monopoly isn't about killing competition, it's about streamlining markets for "efficiency." Let the regulators argue about fairness later; by then, you'll own the regulators too.)
Affirmation #3: *"There's no such thing as enough, just what's next."*
(This one pairs well with any strategic planning session. If your team suggests scaling back, this mantra will refocus them on what really matters: relentless expansion.)

These affirmations aren't just words, they're a mindset. In a billionaire's world, meetings aren't collaborative, they're arenas. Every interaction is a transaction, and your job is to ensure that you're always on the winning side. You aren't negotiating, you're dictating. Collaboration is a myth people tell themselves when they lack the power to take what they want. Your goal is simple: leave every meeting with more than you walked in with, whether that's market share, influence, or someone else's dreams in your pocket.

And don't forget: *"I'm not here to cooperate. I'm here to own."* With these affirmations, every meeting becomes just another opportunity to remind the world that while others debate, you *decide*.

Post-Meeting Affirmations - Take the Win and Move On

The meeting's over, and now it's time to reflect, not on what you could have done better (because let's face it, you were perfect) but on how much closer you are to owning the world. Post-meeting affirmations are all about solidifying your victory, whether you crushed a competitor, forced a merger, or "encouraged" regulators to see things your way. Reflection isn't about self-improvement, it's about reinforcing your dominance. After all, if you don't remind yourself you won, who will? Here are a few affirmations to help you wrap things up like the winner you are.

Affirmation #1: *"I didn't just win, I redefined winning."*
(Perfect for meetings where the competition folded faster than a cheap suit. This reminds you that success isn't just about goals, it's about rewriting the rules in your favor.)
Affirmation #2: *"If they agreed, it's because they feared me."*
(Use this for meetings where everyone smiled and nodded a little too eagerly. Remember, compliance isn't admiration, it's fear, and that's exactly how you like it.)
Affirmation #3: *"Their dreams fuel my reality."*
(Ideal after acquisitions and mergers. Think of it as a poetic reminder that someone's cherished startup was just another building block for your empire.)
Affirmation #4: *"Even when I lose, I win."*
(Perfect for rare moments when the deal didn't go entirely your way. Losing is just a temporary state before your next, larger conquest.)

As you sip your post-meeting drink, whether it's artisanal coffee, champagne, or a protein shake flown in from a glacier-fed spring, take a moment to savor your success. But don't linger too long. Victory isn't about resting on your laurels; it's about moving relentlessly toward the next win. With these affirmations in mind, you can leave every meeting confident that whatever you didn't take today will still be waiting for you tomorrow, ready to be conquered, acquired, or crushed beneath your perfectly polished shoes. Because in the end, the only thing better than winning is knowing there's always more to take.

Affirmations for Public Scandals and Media Scrutiny

Scandals are inevitable when you live life on your own terms, or when your actions accidentally reveal just how indifferent you are to rules and ethics. But fear not! Public outrage is just noise, and the media is a tool waiting to be managed. The goal isn't to avoid scandals; it's to survive and thrive through them. With the right mindset, even the worst headlines can become opportunities. Use these affirmations to center yourself when the masses are howling, journalists are circling, and the Twitter mob is sharpening their pitchforks. Remember: you aren't a villain, you're just misunderstood.

Affirmation #1: "All press is good press, especially if I own the story."
(Perfect for those moments when your name trends for all the wrong reasons. Bad headlines only matter if you let someone else control the narrative. Now's the time to call in favors from the media outlets you definitely don't control, wink, wink.)

Affirmation #2: "Apologies are for the weak; explanations are for winners."
(This mantra is essential when you're pushed to make a public apology. Remember, you're not sorry for what you did, you're sorry that people didn't appreciate your genius. Use vague statements like "I regret any misunderstanding" to keep things hazy.)

Affirmation #3: "History doesn't remember outrage, it remembers winners."
(When the scandal feels overwhelming, remind yourself that today's outrage will be tomorrow's trivia question. They'll forget, but your success will remain forever.)

Affirmation #4: "This isn't a scandal, it's free advertising."
(Use this when critics won't let up. Controversy boosts engagement, and attention—whether good or bad, keeps your brand intact.)

The key to navigating scandal is to stay calm and collected. Public anger is fleeting; your wealth and influence are not. When the media frenzy dies down, and it will, you'll still be standing, richer and stronger than before. Scandals aren't career killers, they're publicity jackpots. Keep these affirmations in your back pocket, and you'll emerge from every controversy with a smirk on your face, another headline conquered, and your empire intact.

End-of-Day Affirmations - Counting Assets, Not Sheep

When the day winds down and it's time to reflect, ordinary people might count their blessings. But not you. You're not in the business of blessings, you're in the business of domination. Instead of sheep, you count assets, acquisitions, and market shares. Your empire doesn't rest, and neither should your mindset. As you lie back in Egyptian cotton sheets, perhaps aboard your private jet or within the walls of your penthouse, it's time to remind yourself that every challenge was just another opportunity, and every small win today brings you one step closer to owning tomorrow. With these affirmations, you'll drift into dreams of conquest and wake ready to claim what's left.

Affirmation #1: *"Every dollar I own works harder than I ever will."*
(Recite this as you review the latest market reports on your tablet before bed. Remember: while others sleep, your money never stops growing.)
Affirmation #2: *"Wealth is infinite, and so is my reach."*
(Use this to relax into the knowledge that there are no limits, just untapped markets and potential acquisitions.)
Affirmation #3: *"Tomorrow belongs to me."*
(This one's great when you need a reminder that the competition is just an obstacle in your inevitable march forward.)

As you settle in, take a moment to mentally list three things you conquered today, perhaps a competitor's market share, a new politician in your pocket, or a PR fire successfully extinguished. Focus not on what you have, but on what's next. There's no such thing as "enough." Contentment is just a speed bump for the complacent. The real thrill isn't in owning, it's in the chase.

If your mind starts to wander toward regrets or second thoughts, cut them off with this simple mantra: *"If it's legal tomorrow, I'll call it innovation today."* There's no time for reflection, only strategy. Close your eyes, envision tomorrow's victories, and feel the satisfaction of knowing that while others sleep, your influence stretches farther. In the billionaire mindset, dreams are just premonitions of success waiting to be realized. With these affirmations guiding you into the night, rest easy, knowing the world is still yours to conquer in the morning.

Advanced Affirmation Practice - Reality Is What You Say It Is

At your level, simple affirmations aren't enough. You don't just repeat mantras, you reshape reality. Laws, markets, and public opinion are malleable if you believe hard enough (and lobby harder). The key to billionaire mastery is learning that reality isn't fixed; it's negotiable. Governments can be persuaded, public outrage can be redirected, and even facts are flexible with enough PR spin. Your power lies in your ability to declare what is true, and, by sheer force of wealth and influence, make it so.

Use these advanced affirmations to ensure that every thought you project becomes the foundation of the world others must live in:

Affirmation #1: *"If I declare it, it becomes true."*
(Say this while planning future market disruptions. Whether it's cryptocurrency or space tourism, your vision shapes the trend.)
Affirmation #2: *"The future bends to my will."*
(This pairs perfectly with strategic meetings about acquisitions or IPOs. Remember: It's not about predicting the future, it's about owning it.)
Affirmation #3: *"If the rules don't fit, I'll rewrite them."*
(Ideal for moments of regulation resistance. Rules are for people without the resources to change them, you have those resources.)
Affirmation #4: *"What they call arrogance, I call foresight."*
(Use this when faced with criticism. Visionaries are often misunderstood, until they own everything in sight.)

The beauty of these affirmations is their simplicity: You don't need to conform to reality, reality conforms to you. If public backlash grows, steer it. If laws tighten, loosen them. If markets shrink, invent a new one. At this level, reality isn't something to be managed, it's something to be manufactured. You're not just playing the game; you're redesigning the board, rearranging the pieces, and, if necessary, setting it all on fire to start anew. You'll soon realize the only limits are the ones others believe in. Reality is just another asset to be acquired, flipped, and sold for a profit. With this mindset, there's no reason to fear failure, because in your world, even failure is just the beginning of a new reality, custom-built for you.

Handling Complaints About 'Alternate Realities' - The Art of Gaslighting with Grace

Some people just don't get it. They'll whine about "facts" and "reality," as if those things haven't always been subjective. They'll call you manipulative, accuse you of gaslighting, and insist that your carefully curated narrative is nothing more than a self-serving fantasy. But let's be honest, these are just the noises of those stuck in an outdated consensus reality. The ones who haven't realized that truth isn't discovered, it's constructed. And if you build it big enough, loud enough, and with enough capital behind it, it becomes the only truth that matters. The complaints of the uninformed shouldn't worry you. You don't need their permission to redefine the rules of existence. When you get accused of manipulating reality to suit your needs, here's how to stay cool, stay collected, and, most importantly, stay on top.

Affirmation #1: *"Gaslighting is just reality management."*
(Perfect for moments when critics accuse you of distorting facts. Spin it: you're not lying—you're shaping perspective.)
Affirmation #2: *"Consensus is for crowds. Reality belongs to leaders."*
(Recite this when journalists or activists demand accountability. The truth isn't what they think it is, it's what you say it is.)
Affirmation #3: *"If they remember things differently, that's their problem."*
(Useful when people claim you've contradicted yourself or shifted your stance. Memories are fluid, and yours is always the correct version.)

Whenever someone pushes back against your "alternate reality," it's important to stay composed. Smile, nod, and then gently pivot the conversation. Call their objections "perceptions" and frame your version as the "bigger picture." Make them question their understanding, not yours. The goal isn't to convince them, you don't need to. The goal is to exhaust them, confuse them, and leave them wondering whether their version of events ever really existed at all. With enough persistence, they'll either accept your narrative or retreat into frustrated silence, both of which are wins for you.

Here's a pro tip: It helps to sprinkle in buzzwords like "perspective," "evolving truth," and "dynamic reality." This makes it sound like you're not distorting facts, you're engaging in sophisticated thinking. And if all else fails, accuse your detractors of being stuck in the past.

Call them rigid or resistant to change. No one wants to be seen as inflexible, and it's often easier for people to go along with your story than to keep fighting against it. In the end, it doesn't matter what *they* think reality is, because, with the right combination of wealth, influence, and PR, your version will always be the one that wins.

Let's Face it

Sometimes the truth needs a little… adjustment. As a billionaire, you can't afford to let facts get in the way of your vision. These "retruths" (or "creative realities") are essential tools for keeping your empire intact and ensuring the masses remain sufficiently dazed and grateful. Whether you're justifying questionable practices, warding off regulations, or explaining away public outrage, these billionaire truths are all you need to keep the narrative working in your favor.

"I'm creating jobs."
Translation: I'm hiring just enough people to keep regulators off my back while underpaying them and automating the rest as soon as possible.
"The market is the best regulator."
Translation: I prefer a world where I can make the rules without interference, and if anyone gets hurt along the way, that's just "market adjustment."
"We all start from the same place."
Translation: I was born with a $10 million trust fund, but I'm sure it was just as hard for me as it is for someone working three jobs to make rent.
"I pay my fair share of taxes."
Translation: I pay exactly what my army of accountants say I can't legally avoid, so technically, that's fair.
"We care deeply about the environment."
Translation: We plant a few trees and buy carbon offsets, but let's not talk about the three private jets I use to "stay agile in global markets."
"Our philanthropy changes the world."
Translation: My charitable foundation is a tax shelter that lets me look generous while maintaining control over how my money gets spent (spoiler: it mostly benefits me).
"If people are unhappy, they should work harder."
Translation: The system I built only works if people never realize it's designed to keep them just desperate enough to stay in line.

"Innovation requires sacrifice."
Translation: That sacrifice is yours, whether it's your job, wages, or sanity, so I can disrupt markets and call it progress.
"Regulation stifles creativity."
Translation: I don't want anyone meddling with my ability to invent new ways of squeezing profits out of labor, data, and loopholes.
"We're all in this together."
Translation: You're all in this together. I'm on my yacht watching the stock market from the middle of the Mediterranean.
"We disrupt industries for the greater good."
Translation: We bulldoze existing industries, crush competitors, and exploit loopholes, then act surprised when people lose jobs and call it progress.
"We're making the world more connected."
Translation: We harvest your personal data and sell it to the highest bidder, but hey, at least your fridge can talk to your toaster now.
"Success is a mindset."
Translation: My mindset involved inheriting millions, leveraging connections, and exploiting labor—something the average person clearly isn't doing right.
"We don't see profits; we see solutions."
Translation: Every problem can be monetized, especially if we create it first and sell the solution later.
"We believe in giving back."
Translation: I give back *control* over my public image, ensure favorable press, and maintain my wealth through philanthropy, all while keeping more than I ever give away.

These "retruths" are vital tools in managing perception and keeping everyone from looking too closely at the underlying system. When repeated enough, by you, your PR team, and every media outlet you can influence, they become indistinguishable from facts. Reality isn't just what people believe, it's what you convince them to believe. And if that reality works for you? Well, isn't that the only truth that matters?

The Ultimate Billionaire Affirmation - "Because I Can"

At the end of the day, all the affirmations, mantras, and retruths boil down to a single, unassailable truth: *"Because I can."* This isn't just a fallback, it's the north star of billionaire philosophy. Why did you launch a vanity space program? Because you can. Why lay off half your workforce while buying another private jet? Because you can. Why not pay taxes? Because, obviously, you can. The beauty of this affirmation is that it requires no justification. It needs no moral dressing or strategic spin. It's a pure, raw acknowledgment of the power you wield and the reality you shape.

Recite this mantra whenever someone questions your motives, decisions, or actions. It works in every situation, whether you're defending a massive tax dodge, justifying a $500 million yacht, or announcing a 30% price hike for a life-saving drug. There's no need to explain yourself. Remember: if someone else had your power, they'd do the same, or at least, they wish they could. This affirmation is your get-out-of-guilt-free card, your final word in any argument. It's not a defense, but a declaration that you exist beyond rules, ethics, or public opinion.

Use Case Example:
Reporter: *"Why did you cut benefits for workers earning minimum wage while giving yourself a $50 million bonus?"*
You: *"Because I can."*
(Smile gently. Mic drop.)

Once you embrace *"Because I can,"* you free yourself from the burdens of accountability. Empathy is irrelevant, fairness is for the naive, and public outrage is just background noise. All that matters is that you have the power to do what you want, and no one, not politicians, journalists, or protestors, can stop you. This is the ultimate affirmation, the mantra that renders all other justifications obsolete.

So, as you stand at the top of your empire, survey all that you own, and contemplate tomorrow's acquisitions, remind yourself: *"Because I can."* And that, billionaire, is the only truth that matters.

Special Note: The Language of Manipulation – Billionaire Edition

Going Forward, Remember *These* Words

Language is a powerful tool, and billionaires know this better than anyone. In their hands, words become weapons, used to distort reality, suppress dissent, and keep us all too busy dreaming of riches to question how the game is rigged. This isn't just exaggeration; it's Orwellian manipulation. Take phrases like "job creators" or "wealth trickles down." These aren't neutral descriptions, they're crafted fictions, designed to make us see billionaires as benevolent forces of good, rather than the ruthless accumulators of wealth and power they really are. By rebranding greed as "innovation" and exploitation as "opportunity," they twist language into a smokescreen, one that keeps the public pacified and hopeful for a future that's statistically out of reach. We're sold the idea that the American Dream is alive and well, that if we just work hard enough, we too might someday be at the top. But look around: the billionaire dream is a mirage, accessible to almost no one, and yet it continues to loom over us as a beacon of "possibility." This is language abused, a story sold to keep us in line, content with the crumbs.

Be cautious, because words do matter, and those in power know how to wield them like scalpels, cutting reality into convenient pieces that serve their agendas. Consider phrases like "personal responsibility" or "self-made," which suggest that failure to succeed lies solely with the individual. By pushing narratives that emphasize individual effort and downplay systemic barriers, billionaires make us believe that poverty, lack of healthcare, or homelessness are personal shortcomings rather than symptoms of a deeply flawed system. They frame their astronomical wealth as a sign of merit, a reward for hard work, rather than the outcome of systems built to favor them at every turn. This language isn't accidental, it's strategic, designed to keep us idolizing them instead of questioning them. If we don't recognize this manipulation, we risk internalizing it, accepting their definitions and their dreams as our own, and losing sight of the world we could build if we dared to see through their words.

Chapter 2
The Art of Hoarding

The Hoarders Creed- Why Sharing is Overrated

Sharing is for amateurs, the gullible, and those still clinging to the fantasy that life is about fairness or community. You, dear billionaire, have transcended those primitive instincts. Sharing is a relic of childhood lessons, a naïve ideology fed to the masses to keep them docile while the world's true players, people like you, amass the resources that truly matter. The hoarder's creed is simple: if it can be owned, it must be owned. Land, money, power, influence, these aren't just assets; they're trophies, each one a testament to your dominance. Sharing? That's just a way for the less ambitious to beg for scraps while calling it morality. Let's get one thing straight: your wealth isn't just about having more, it's about ensuring everyone else has less. After all, what's the point of hoarding billions if it doesn't come with the satisfaction of seeing others struggle to scrape by? You've worked (or inherited, or exploited) too much to let the concept of "enough" enter your vocabulary. Enough is for people who don't dream big enough, who haven't learned that the true thrill isn't in spending wealth, it's in stockpiling it, watching the numbers climb like a game you can't lose. Sharing disrupts this beautiful cycle. If you share, you're giving up control, and control is everything.

But let's not get emotional about this. Sharing isn't just overrated, it's inefficient. When you share, you dilute power. Imagine splitting an estate, a fortune, or even an idea. Suddenly, your pristine empire becomes tainted with compromise, with others thinking they have a say. Collaboration sounds noble, but it's a slippery slope to relinquishing what's rightfully yours. Why let others in when you can just keep taking, quietly tightening your grip on every facet of the system? Sharing breeds dependency, and dependency breeds entitlement. If people think you're generous, they'll keep coming back for more, like stray cats you fed once who now expect a banquet. The masses will tell you that sharing creates community, that it's the foundation of trust and progress. But the truth is, sharing only works for those who have nothing to lose. For you, sharing is a liability, a crack in the dam that holds your wealth and power. If you share, even a little, the floodgates will open, and soon people will think they're entitled to your billions. They'll start whispering about redistribution, about fairness, about how "no one needs that much money." This, of course, is nonsense. You earned, or inherited, or manipulated, what you have. Your success isn't an accident; it's a natural law, proof that the strongest rise to the top. Sharing undermines that narrative, suggesting you owe bupkis to the world simply because you live in it.

Let's consider a scenario. Say you decide to "share" a portion of your wealth to fund public programs. You build a school, a hospital, maybe even a park. Sounds harmless, right? But what happens next? The public starts expecting more. Suddenly, your name on the building isn't enough. They want you to pay living wages, to stop lobbying against regulations, to consider the "greater good." The demands never end. Sharing is a slippery slope, and once you start, there's no going back. The better strategy is to feign sharing, philanthropy is your friend here. Announce a generous donation, smile for the cameras, and let your PR team handle the details. Meanwhile, you keep your wealth firmly in your grasp, untouchable and intact.

Sharing also creates the illusion of equality, and let's be honest, equality is bad for business. If everyone has the same opportunities, the same resources, the same shot at success, the system crumbles. You thrive on inequality, it's the engine of your empire. When people are struggling, they're too busy surviving to question why you have so much. Sharing destabilizes this delicate balance, giving them just enough power to start asking uncomfortable questions. Why does one person need so much wealth? Why are billionaires celebrated while children starve? Sharing opens the door to these conversations, and that's a risk you can't afford to take.

So, repeat this mantra whenever someone suggests you "give back": *"I don't owe the world anything."* Your wealth is yours to keep, hoard, and grow. Sharing is a quaint idea, suitable for kindergarteners and socialists, but not for you. You didn't climb to the top to hand out pieces of the pie; you climbed to own the bakery. Sharing is overrated, unnecessary, and, most importantly, dangerous to your continued dominance. The hoarder's creed isn't just about greed, it's about survival. It's about understanding that in a world of limited resources, the one who hoards the most wins. Remember, billionaire: the less you share, the more you control. And in the end, control, not community, is the real currency of power.

Feng Shui Your Fortune- Turning excess wealth into an aesthetic

Wealth isn't just power, it's an art form. When you've accumulated more money than most small countries, the challenge isn't how to spend it; it's how to display it. This is where the philosophy of *feng shui for billionaires* comes into play: transforming your excess fortune into an aesthetic that projects dominance, sophistication, and effortless superiority. Regular feng shui focuses on energy flow, harmony, and balance. Billionaire feng shui? It's about ensuring your wealth screams louder than anyone else's, subtly (or not so subtly) reminding everyone that you own the room, the building, and maybe the land it's on. Let's start with the basics. A billionaire's environment should reflect the size of their fortune, but not in a gaudy, lottery-winner way. Tasteful excess is the goal. Think sleek private jets with hand-stitched leather seats, penthouses decorated with priceless contemporary art, and yachts that double as floating museums. Your spaces should radiate power, quiet, commanding, and unmistakable. Remember, money talks, but it shouldn't shout. A mansion dripping with gold chandeliers and marble everything is trying too hard; a minimalist estate with invisible technology and a subtle $20 million painting casually hung in the guest bathroom? That's class.

Placement matters. In traditional feng shui, objects are positioned to create positive energy flow. In billionaire feng shui, placement is about projecting dominance. Your most expensive pieces, think rare art, custom furniture, or that $100,000 coffee table made from a single piece of petrified wood, should be strategically located to ensure maximum impact. The goal isn't just to impress guests but to intimidate them. They shouldn't just see your wealth; they should *feel* it, like an atmospheric pressure drop when they walk into your living room. Your possessions should tell a story, one of unassailable success and effortless superiority. For instance, that antique Persian rug wasn't just expensive; it came with a story about how you outbid a rival billionaire to acquire it. Those rare books in your library? You don't read them, they're there to project intellectual depth (or at least suggest you employ someone who does). Every item should serve a dual purpose: as an aesthetic choice and as a trophy of your ability to possess what others cannot.

Let's talk about rooms. Each space in your home, office, or yacht should reflect a different facet of your empire. The dining room isn't just for eating, it's where deals are sealed. A table made from reclaimed ancient oak, chairs upholstered in leather flown in from Tuscany, and a chandelier crafted by a glassblower who only takes two commissions a year, this isn't dining, it's theater. The study? It's where you display rare first editions and trophies from your "philanthropy," like plaques from universities that are happy to rename a building after you. Your wine cellar isn't just stocked; it's curated, featuring vintages that require an app to translate their labels. Remember: nothing is random. Everything should convey intention, purpose, and power. Let's not forget the outdoors. Your gardens and exteriors should rival public landmarks, with landscaping that requires a team of 20 just to maintain. Think sculpted hedges, koi ponds imported from Japan, and infinity pools that stretch so far they look like they're swallowing the horizon. And if you're truly committed to the aesthetic, why not a private island? Nothing says "untouchable" like owning land where you make the rules.

But feng shui for billionaires isn't just about what you own, it's about how you control the space around you. Wealth isn't static; it's dynamic, a constantly flowing river of acquisitions and upgrades. That's why your aesthetic must evolve. Don't be afraid to refresh your collection every few years. Auction off yesterday's treasures to the merely wealthy (a satisfying reminder of your superiority) and replace them with something even rarer, even more unattainable. Your aesthetic is your armor, your way of telling the world, "This is what winning looks like." Critics may call this wasteful, a grotesque display of greed in a world rife with inequality. That's fine. They're supposed to criticize, you're supposed to win. The point isn't to justify your excess; it's to make it undeniable. When the masses walk through a museum and see the painting you lent for exhibit, they'll know it's just on loan, a casual flex of your cultural dominance. Your wealth isn't just money; it's your legacy, written in marble, gold, and priceless artifacts.

So, billionaire, arrange your empire with intention. Turn your fortune into a fortress of aesthetic dominance. Let your wealth speak, not just in numbers, but in the quiet, crushing weight of objects so rare, so unattainable, that they cease to be things and become symbols. This is your world. Feng shui it well.

Avoiding the Guilt Trap- Techniques for justifying hoarding while looking philanthropic

Guilt is the Achilles' heel of power, and as a billionaire, you simply can't afford it. Not because it might lead to self-reflection, heavens, no, but because guilt can make you vulnerable. If you let guilt take root, it becomes a crack in the fortress of your wealth, a weak point that critics and protesters can exploit. That's why it's essential to not only suppress guilt but to weaponize it, to turn it into an opportunity to reinforce your image as a benevolent titan. By mastering the art of appearing philanthropic without actually disrupting your empire of hoarding, you'll not only avoid the guilt trap but use it to your advantage.

Step 1: Redefine Philanthropy as Investment

Let's be clear: philanthropy isn't about giving, it's about positioning. Forget charity as a selfless act; think of it as a PR strategy with excellent ROI. When the masses see your name attached to a hospital wing, a museum, or a university program, they don't think about how much you kept for yourself, they only see what you gave. The key is to attach your name to high-profile projects that provide maximum visibility while requiring minimal sacrifice. Naming rights are your best friend. A "generous donation" that only accounts for 0.0001% of your net worth but earns you a plaque, a photo-op, and glowing headlines? That's philanthropy done right.

But don't stop there. You can leverage your philanthropic ventures for financial gain. Foundations are perfect for this. Set one up, funnel some capital into it, and use it as a vehicle to support causes that align with your business interests. Want to look green while expanding your oil empire? Donate to renewable energy research that conveniently partners with your company. Interested in shaping public opinion? Fund think tanks that generate studies favorable to your industry. With the right framing, philanthropy isn't just an expense, it's an investment in your narrative and your bottom line.

Step 2: Create the Illusion of Generosity

When you're a billionaire, perception is everything. The goal isn't to solve problems, it's to look like you care about solving them. Start by embracing the power of vague announcements. Pledge millions, better yet, billions, to causes without specifying when, where, or how the money will be distributed. Words like "pledge" and "commit" are your allies here because they sound concrete while remaining entirely flexible.

Another strategy is to focus on symbolic gestures. For instance, donate a few million to a cause that generates emotional headlines, disaster relief, child hunger, or medical research. The sum might seem large to the average person, but to you, it's pocket change. The beauty of this technique is that the public doesn't see the percentage of your wealth you're donating, they only see the dollar amount, which always seems impressive to those who've never seen a billion.

Step 3: Control the Narrative

Philanthropy isn't about what you do, it's about what people think you're doing. To that end, you must control the story from the start. Employ a team of PR professionals who specialize in spinning your generosity into an epic saga of heroism. Words like "visionary," "trailblazer," and "world-changer" should appear in every press release. Own the media narrative by partnering with outlets willing to highlight your contributions while conveniently ignoring your tax avoidance schemes or labor practices.

Don't forget to use social media to your advantage. A single post about your latest charitable initiative, accompanied by a photo of you looking concerned yet hopeful, can generate thousands of likes, shares, and glowing comments. Public gratitude is addictive, and it reinforces your image as someone who *cares* deeply about the world's problems, even if you're the one profiting from them.

Step 4: Shift Responsibility

One of the best ways to avoid guilt is to convince yourself, and everyone else, that your wealth isn't the problem. Use your philanthropy to frame societal issues as challenges that require collective action. For example, donate to educational programs and emphasize that education, not economic reform, is the key to solving inequality. This subtly shifts the focus away from systemic issues (like wealth hoarding) and onto individual effort. It's a win-win: you look generous while deflecting attention from the real causes of the problem.

You can also use your philanthropy to redirect blame. Fund initiatives that address symptoms rather than causes, soup kitchens instead of wage reform, scholarships instead of affordable tuition. This ensures that you're seen as part of the solution without ever threatening the structures that made you wealthy in the first place.

Step 5: Establish Emotional Distance

Guilt often arises from empathy, and empathy is a luxury you can't afford. To avoid falling into the guilt trap, establish emotional distance from the people your philanthropy is supposedly helping. Never interact directly with recipients. Let intermediaries handle the distribution of funds and focus on the big picture, preferably from a yacht or private jet.

If guilt does creep in, reframe your perspective. Remind yourself that your success benefits society in countless ways. The jobs you create, the taxes you don't pay (but could have), and the inspiration you provide to future entrepreneurs, all of these are contributions that outweigh any minor inconveniences caused by your hoarding. Repeat this mantra: *"I've earned this, and the world is better for it."*

Step 6: Never Stop Hoarding

Finally, remember that philanthropy is a tool, not a goal. The ultimate aim is to protect your wealth, not distribute it. Every charitable act should serve to solidify your position, enhance your reputation, and deflect criticism. Hoarding isn't just a habit, it's a way of life, and philanthropy is just another means to justify it.

So, billionaire, avoid the guilt trap by mastering these techniques. Philanthropy doesn't have to disrupt your hoarding, it can enhance it. With the right strategy, you can look like a hero while staying firmly in control of the empire you've built. In the end, it's not about how much you give, it's about how much you keep.

Asset Expansion as a Spiritual Practice- More yachts, more joy

Forget yoga, meditation, or mindfulness—true enlightenment comes from the acquisition of assets. When you're a billionaire, expanding your empire isn't just about increasing your wealth; it's a form of spiritual practice. Each new yacht, private jet, or sprawling estate isn't just another indulgence, it's a testament to your divine ability to manifest abundance in a world of scarcity. For you, asset expansion is about more than materialism; it's a journey of self-discovery, a path to proving that your wealth is both boundless and justified.

Let's start with yachts, the holy grail of billionaire enlightenment. A yacht isn't just a boat—it's a floating temple to your success. It's where you can meditate on your greatness while sipping champagne in a hot tub that overlooks the ocean. Owning one yacht is impressive, but true spiritual growth comes from owning several, each more extravagant than the last. Your smaller yacht can dock inside your larger yacht, a physical representation of your wealth's infinite layers. Add a submarine and a helicopter to the mix, not for practicality, but because you can. Each additional feature is a mantra, a way of affirming that you deserve everything you desire, no matter how unnecessary it may seem to others.

Real estate is another essential element of your spiritual journey. Why have one home when you can have dozens? A penthouse in New York for meetings, a château in the French countryside for "downtime," a villa in Tuscany for wine weekends, every property adds another layer to your aura of untouchable success. These homes aren't just investments; they're reflections of your soul, each one carefully curated to remind the world that you are above its petty concerns. And don't forget the private island, your ultimate sanctuary, a place where you can achieve the nirvana of absolute privacy while watching the sun set over land that belongs only to you.

Private jets are the wings of your spiritual practice. Commercial flights are for mere mortals; you, on the other hand, glide above the clouds in luxury. Your jet isn't just a means of transportation, it's a statement. Gold-plated fixtures, handwoven carpets, and a custom wine cellar at 30,000 feet aren't indulgences, they're necessities. After all, how can you contemplate your next acquisition if you're stuck in coach with the commoners? Each takeoff is a metaphor for your rising power, each landing a reminder that you've arrived in every possible sense of the word.

Art is the final frontier of asset expansion. Buying rare paintings and sculptures isn't about appreciating beauty, it's about owning a piece of history. When you bid on a Van Gogh or a Picasso, you're not just buying art; you're buying immortality. Every time your name appears in the catalog of an auction house, it's another prayer answered in the religion of wealth. Collecting art isn't just about showcasing your taste, it's about reminding the world that you can afford what others can only dream of. Your collection is your legacy, a gallery of your dominance over time, culture, and scarcity itself.

Critics may call this greed, but they fail to see the deeper meaning. Asset expansion isn't about hoarding, it's about fulfillment. Every new acquisition is a reminder that you've transcended the limits of ordinary life. Where others struggle for meaning, you find it in the weight of your gold-plated paperweights, the shine of your diamond-encrusted watches, and the purr of your fleet of luxury cars. You're not accumulating for the sake of accumulation; you're practicing abundance as an art form, proving that true happiness comes not from letting go, but from grabbing hold of everything in sight.

And don't let anyone guilt you into thinking otherwise. The masses might complain about wealth inequality or call your acquisitions "excessive," but that's just their lack of enlightenment talking. If they truly understood the spiritual practice of asset expansion, they'd thank you for demonstrating what's possible. By owning so much, you're showing the world that limits are illusions. You're not just living life, you're mastering it, proving that happiness isn't found in simplicity but in the sheer, unrelenting pursuit of more.

So, billionaire, embrace asset expansion as your spiritual path. Let each new yacht, jet, and estate bring you closer to your true self. Don't question the morality of your acquisitions, revel in them. Each new asset is a meditation, a celebration, and a declaration of your worth. More yachts, more joy. More assets, more enlightenment. In the end, the only true sin is having less than you could.

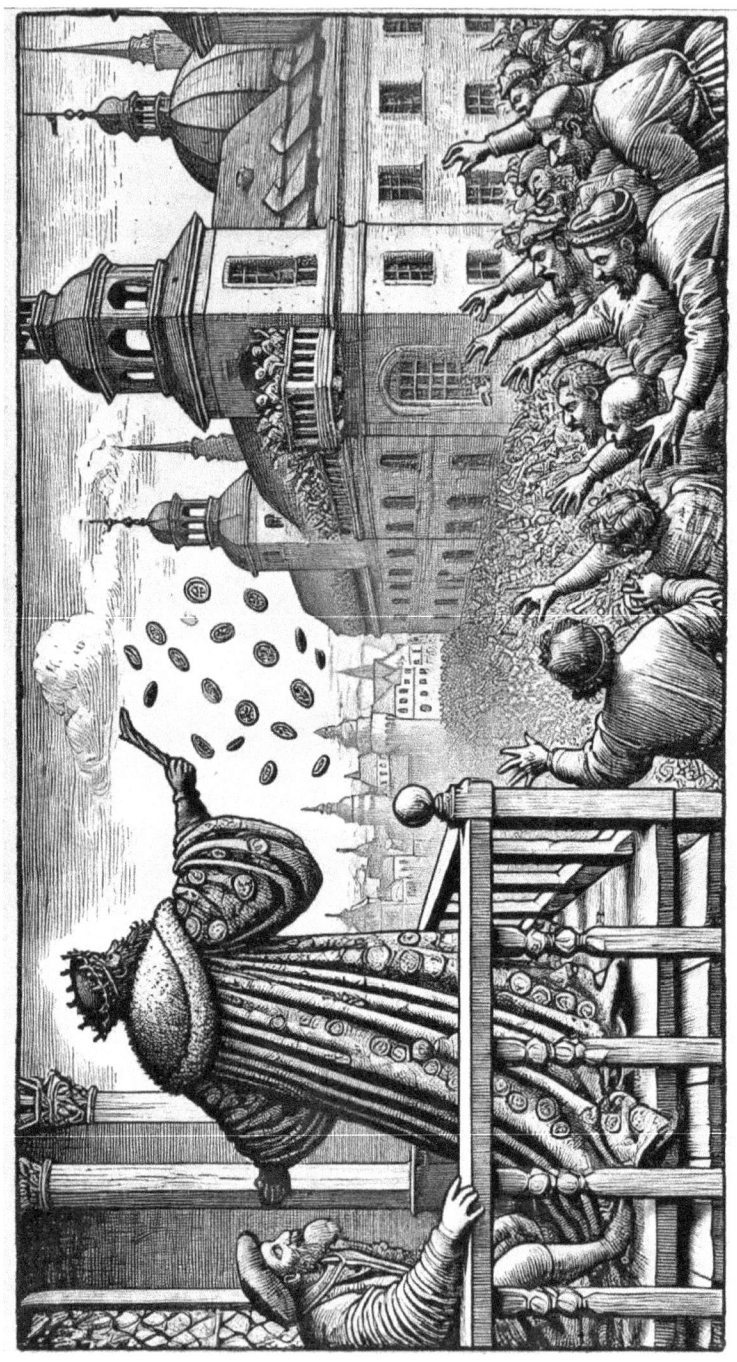

Chapter 3
Faking Philanthropy

Charity or Tax Haven? Why foundations are billionaire shields

Let's get one thing straight: foundations aren't just tools for doing good, they're fortresses for protecting wealth. To the public, they're noble monuments to your generosity, shining examples of your commitment to "giving back." But behind the gilded façade, foundations serve a much more practical purpose: shielding your fortune from taxes, critics, and anyone foolish enough to demand accountability. They are the ultimate billionaire cheat code, allowing you to maintain the appearance of altruism while keeping your empire intact and untouched.

Here's how it works. When you set up a foundation, you're not "giving away" your money; you're simply relocating it to a safe, tax-advantaged environment that you still control. Foundations are technically separate entities, but don't be fooled by legal jargon, they're yours to wield. You decide where the money goes, how it's spent, and who benefits. The beauty of this arrangement is that while your wealth is ostensibly dedicated to charity, it remains insulated from pesky things like taxes, government oversight, or redistribution. It's like moving your assets into a castle with a moat and calling it a community center. The public, of course, sees only the surface. They don't understand that a foundation is as much about optics as it is about impact. When critics accuse you of hoarding wealth, you can point to your foundation as evidence of your benevolence. The media will cover your "transformative contributions," and any mention of your tax avoidance will be buried beneath headlines celebrating your generosity. The trick is to ensure your foundation appears active and effective while keeping its actual spending to a minimum. Remember: perception is everything.

Take donations, for example. Foundations often commit to giving away money over long periods, decades, even centuries. This ensures that the total amount pledged sounds enormous while the actual outflow is carefully controlled. Pledging $10 billion sounds groundbreaking, but if it's spread out over 50 years, it's less than the interest your fortune accrues in a month. Meanwhile, the foundation itself employs a team of accountants and legal experts to ensure that every dollar spent maximizes your PR returns while minimizing your tax obligations. It's philanthropy on paper, but in practice, it's business as usual. Foundations also allow you to fund causes that align with your personal or corporate interests. Want to combat climate change without sacrificing profits from your oil company? Fund "green initiatives" that focus on theoretical solutions rather than regulations. Want to support education while ensuring your industry remains dominant? Endow scholarships that funnel students into fields beneficial to your bottom line. This is strategic philanthropy: spending money to ensure the system remains favorable to you, all while earning applause for your "visionary" efforts.

And let's not forget the perks. Foundations allow you to wield influence in ways that benefit you directly. By funding think tanks, research institutions, and policy initiatives, you can shape public opinion and legislation to align with your interests. Need favorable coverage in the press? Donate to a journalism fund. Want to maintain political connections? Sponsor events attended by lawmakers. Foundations aren't just about protecting your wealth, they're about expanding your power, all under the guise of doing good. Of course, there will always be skeptics who see through the charade. Some will point out that your foundation is essentially a vanity project, designed more to glorify you than to solve real problems. Others will argue that your wealth wouldn't exist without the systemic inequalities your foundation claims to address. But don't worry, those voices are easily drowned out by the roar of your PR machine. With the right messaging, you can make anyone who questions your motives look like a bitter cynic. You, on the other hand, are a philanthropist, a visionary, a leader. At least, that's what the press releases say.

So, billionaire, embrace the foundation as your ultimate shield. Use it to protect your fortune, enhance your reputation, and deflect criticism. Let it serve as both a symbol of your "generosity" and a fortress for your wealth. After all, true philanthropy isn't about giving, it's about controlling the narrative. In the world of billionaire charity, the appearance of altruism is often more powerful than the act itself. Play your cards right, and your foundation will be your greatest asset, not because it gives, but because it lets you keep.

The Optics of Generosity: How to Make Minimal Donations Look Maximal

When you're a billionaire, generosity isn't about the size of your donation, it's about the perception of your donation. The art of appearing generous lies in making the smallest possible contributions seem like monumental acts of altruism. You don't need to actually solve any problems; you just need people to believe you're trying. By mastering the optics of generosity, you can maintain your wealth, bolster your reputation, and shield yourself from criticism, all while barely lifting a financial finger.

The Illusion of Scale

The secret to maximizing the appearance of generosity lies in exploiting numbers. Pledge large amounts over long periods, ensuring the total figure grabs headlines while the yearly disbursement is barely a dent in your wealth. For example, announcing a $1 billion pledge to fight climate change sounds groundbreaking. What the public won't notice is that the money will be distributed over 20 years, with annual payments amounting to less than the cost of maintaining your third yacht. The key is to focus on the headline figure. Few people will read the fine print, and even fewer will question it. Don't forget to use percentages to your advantage. By donating a fraction of your net worth—say 0.01%—you can create the illusion of significant sacrifice. Most people can't fathom the scale of a billion dollars, so even a relatively small sum seems astronomical. To the average person, a $10 million donation looks heroic, despite the fact that it's less than a rounding error in your financial portfolio.

High-Impact Announcements, Low-Impact Results

Perception is everything. When making a donation, the actual impact of your money isn't nearly as important as the announcement itself. Carefully stage the moment for maximum visibility. A press conference with a tearful recipient, a photo of you shaking hands with community leaders, or even a video of the "transformative impact" your funds will supposedly have—these are the tools of the trade. The public doesn't want to see spreadsheets or detailed plans; they want emotional narratives. Give them what they crave, and they'll never think to ask why your donation didn't really move the needle. For extra flair, consider pledging to causes that are abstract or long-term, like "curing cancer" or "ending poverty." These ambitious goals make you look visionary, even if the funds are so thinly distributed that they accomplish nothing. Remember, the vaguer the mission, the harder it is for anyone to hold you accountable for results.

Timing Is Everything

Strategic timing can amplify the impact of even the smallest donation. Are you facing public criticism for questionable business practices? Announce a generous contribution to a popular cause. Did a scandal involving your company hit the news cycle? Quickly "give back" to the community with a well-publicized donation. Timing donations to coincide with moments of scrutiny is an excellent way to redirect attention and reshape the narrative. Suddenly, you're not the villain, you're the hero. If you really want to stretch the optics, commit to a pledge during times of public crisis. Disaster relief donations are particularly effective. A few million dollars toward hurricane recovery or wildfire aid can make you look like a savior, even if the money barely scratches the surface of what's needed. The urgency of these moments ensures you'll dominate the headlines, overshadowing the fact that your contribution is a drop in the bucket compared to your wealth.

Collaborate for Amplified Glory

Another trick is to pool resources with other billionaires. Collaborative pledges allow you to inflate the total amount while reducing your individual contribution. A group of 20 billionaires pledging $100 million collectively sounds impressive, but your personal share might be less than what you spend on maintaining your private island. Collaboration not only spreads the financial burden but also creates the illusion of a unified movement, making you seem like a team player rather than a self-interested mogul.

Additionally, partnering with existing organizations can enhance the optics. By working with a respected charity, you borrow their credibility and gain access to their audience. Let the charity handle the heavy lifting while you reap the PR benefits. This approach not only minimizes your effort but also ensures that your donation looks larger than it really is.

Leverage Media Coverage

The power of a donation lies in its story. Invest in PR teams and media consultants who specialize in turning your contributions into compelling narratives. Make sure the media knows about your donation well in advance so they can prepare glowing coverage. Buzzwords like "transformative," "groundbreaking," and "unprecedented" should appear in every headline. The goal is to make people believe your contribution is changing the world, even if it's barely changing your financial statement. Use social media to amplify your message. Post photos, share personal reflections, and thank the public for allowing you the "privilege" of giving back. Engage directly with followers who praise your generosity, it'll reinforce the idea that you're approachable and humble, even as you sit in a mansion worth more than most people will earn in their lifetime.

Avoid the Hard Questions

Be prepared for skeptics who might question why you're not giving more. The best way to disarm them is with humility and deflection. Statements like, "This is just the beginning" or "We're working to identify additional opportunities" create the impression that more is on the way, even if it isn't. If pressed about why you're not tackling the root causes of systemic issues, pivot to talking about the "complexity" of the problems. This reinforces the idea that you're doing your best in a challenging world, rather than avoiding real solutions to protect your wealth.

The Bottom Line

The optics of generosity are about doing just enough to maintain the appearance of compassion while preserving your fortune. By leveraging timing, collaboration, media coverage, and strategic announcements, you can make minimal contributions look monumental. Remember: it's not about what you give, it's about what people *think* you've given. With the right narrative, even a modest donation can make you look like the savior of humanity. And at the end of the day, isn't that the most valuable asset of all?

Naming Rights: Why Nothing Says "I Care" Like Your Name on a Building

When it comes to philanthropy, few strategies are as effective, or as satisfying, as slapping your name on a building. Naming rights are the ultimate win-win: they make you look generous while ensuring your legacy is quite literally etched in stone. A hospital wing, a university library, or even a city park named after you becomes a permanent advertisement for your benevolence, regardless of how little you actually gave to make it happen. After all, what better way to show you "care" than by branding a public good as your personal achievement?

The beauty of naming rights lies in their simplicity. You're not funding systemic change; you're funding a structure. It doesn't matter if the building's operations are underfunded, its staff underpaid, or its purpose barely fulfilled, what matters is that your name is prominently displayed for generations to come. To the public, your name on a children's hospital says "compassion," even if your donation was a fraction of your annual tax savings. The optics are priceless, and the cost is negligible in billionaire terms.

For maximum impact, choose institutions with high visibility and cultural cachet. Universities are ideal because they churn out graduates who will associate your name with prestige for decades. Museums are another favorite, offering you a place in the arts without requiring you to actually create anything. Even public parks can be an option, especially if they include a tasteful plaque detailing your "unwavering commitment to the community."

At the end of the day, naming rights are about controlling the narrative. They allow you to rewrite your public image as a benefactor and visionary, no matter how ruthless your business practices may be. Your name doesn't just adorn a building, it replaces criticism with admiration. Because in the world of billionaire philanthropy, perception is everything.

When to Donate Just Enough: Deflecting Criticism with Well-Timed Gifts

Sometimes, even billionaires face the pesky nuisance of public outrage. A scandal erupts, an exploitative practice comes to light, or maybe the media finally notices your offshore accounts. Whatever the cause, the solution is simple: a well-timed, strategically modest donation. You don't need to give away a fortune, just enough to change the narrative and shift the focus from your misdeeds to your "generosity."

The key is timing. Your donation should hit the news cycle when criticism is at its peak, creating a tidal wave of positive headlines to drown out the negativity. Facing accusations of union-busting? Announce a multi-million-dollar commitment to job training programs. Caught lobbying against climate regulations? Donate to renewable energy research. The beauty of this strategy is that you don't actually need to change your behavior, just the conversation. The public is remarkably forgiving when there's a feel-good story to latch onto.

The amount you donate doesn't have to be significant by billionaire standards. A few million dollars is more than enough to impress the masses, especially when the gift is tied to an emotional cause like disaster relief, hunger, or education. The goal isn't to solve the problem but to appear as though you care deeply about solving it. Make sure to frame your contribution as part of a larger "commitment" to social good. Words like "dedicated," "compassionate," and "visionary" should dominate the press release.

Finally, don't forget to milk the PR value. Pair your announcement with a heartfelt speech, a social media post, or a photo of you surrounded by smiling beneficiaries. People won't notice, or care, that your donation is a drop in the ocean compared to your wealth. What they'll remember is the image of you as a hero, saving the day when it mattered most. And that's the real gift: protecting your reputation without breaking a sweat.

Chapter 4
Networking on Super Yachts

Yachts as Power Moves- Why Sea-Level Exclusivity Matters

Owning a yacht isn't just about luxury, it's about dominance. At sea, there's no traffic, no crowds, and no neighbors to infringe upon your personal sovereignty. Yachts are the ultimate status symbols, floating fortresses of exclusivity that proclaim, "I've transcended landlocked limitations." For billionaires, yachts aren't indulgences; they're power moves. They're where deals are struck, alliances are forged, and rivalries are quietly measured by the length of the hull and the amenities on board. Sea-level exclusivity isn't just a perk of wealth, it's a necessity for those who want to truly rule.

The Statement of Ownership

A yacht isn't just a boat; it's a statement. It tells the world that you're not confined by geography or ordinary rules of travel. Your yacht is your mobile kingdom, a place where you call the shots—literally and figuratively. The size and features of your yacht are direct reflections of your standing in the billionaire hierarchy. A 150-foot vessel might impress the nouveau riche, but true titans of industry need something in the 300-foot range, complete with helipads, submarines, and pools that rival landlocked resorts. It's not just about having a yacht, it's about having the yacht.

The Practical Power of Isolation

Yachts provide an unparalleled level of exclusivity. At sea, you control who enters your domain. There are no reporters lurking around corners, no uninvited guests, and no protesters holding signs. Meetings held on a yacht are secure and private, away from prying eyes and ears. This isolation makes them ideal venues for discussing sensitive deals or hashing out mergers without interference. Aboard your vessel, you're untouchable, a floating reminder that you exist above the fray of ordinary life.

The Social Currency of Yacht Ownership

Yachts aren't just for solitude, they're social tools. The invitations you extend to your yacht signal status and exclusivity. Hosting a soirée aboard your vessel isn't just a party, it's a demonstration of power. Guests aren't just attending an event; they're stepping into your world, where you control the environment, the ambiance, and, by extension, the relationships. Aboard your yacht, you set the tone, whether it's a relaxed cocktail hour with understated opulence or a full-scale extravaganza designed to leave your peers in awe. Networking is a game, and yachts are the ultimate playing field. Events like the Monaco Yacht Show or exclusive regattas aren't just social gatherings, they're opportunities to solidify alliances and size up rivals. The billionaire elite use their yachts to host discreet meetings with political leaders, potential business partners, and celebrities, all under the guise of leisure. These events are where billionaires cement their influence, broker deals, and remind each other who truly holds the reins of power.

The Competitive Edge

Yacht ownership is inherently competitive. Every feature, from the materials used to construct the hull to the onboard amenities, is an opportunity to one-up the competition. Your yacht is a stage for your success, a physical representation of your superiority. A larger deck, a more advanced navigation system, or an onboard concert hall isn't just an indulgence; it's a declaration. The competition doesn't end at size, design, innovation, and exclusivity all play a role. A yacht equipped with a state-of-the-art desalination plant and its own ecosystem isn't just a marvel; it's a flex.

Environmental Virtue Signaling

While yachts are notoriously resource-intensive, modern billionaires know how to spin the narrative. A "green" yacht, outfitted with solar panels or hybrid engines, allows you to sail guilt-free, or at least appear to. Claiming environmental consciousness adds another layer to your image: not only are you successful, but you're also forward-thinking and responsible. It's the perfect way to deflect criticism while continuing to enjoy the perks of your floating empire.

The Subtle Art of Schmoozing Billionaires- Turning Acquaintances into Allies

In the world of billionaires, relationships aren't built, they're brokered. Schmoozing is the currency of influence, and knowing how to navigate the delicate dance of flattery, collaboration, and mutual benefit is essential to turning casual acquaintances into powerful allies. The goal isn't just to make connections; it's to strategically align yourself with individuals who can elevate your status, expand your empire, or serve as valuable buffers when public criticism comes knocking. Schmoozing isn't about friendship, it's about leverage.

Step 1: Choose Your Targets Wisely

Not all billionaires are created equal, and not all are worth your time. Identify those whose resources, influence, or networks can complement your own. A tech mogul might open doors to innovative industries, while an oil tycoon could provide access to untapped global markets. Focus on those who can help you achieve your long-term goals. Schmoozing isn't about making friends, it's about making moves.

Step 2: Flattery Is a Science

Billionaires love being admired, but it's crucial to flatter them without being obvious. Research their achievements and interests, then weave subtle compliments into conversations. Mention their latest philanthropic initiative, marvel at their business foresight, or ask for advice on a challenge you're facing (one you've already solved, of course). The key is to make them feel respected and valued without coming off as insincere. Ego is your entry point, handle it delicately, and doors will open.

Step 3: Create a Sense of Exclusivity

Billionaires thrive on exclusivity, so make them feel like your attention is rare and valuable. Don't seem too eager; instead, cultivate an air of effortless charm. Be someone they want to impress. Attend the right events—elite galas, yacht parties, and private summits—and position yourself as an equal, not a subordinate. Proximity matters; the closer you are to their inner circle, the more likely you are to gain their trust and favor.

Step 4: Find Mutual Interests

Every billionaire has hobbies, from collecting rare art to funding obscure space projects. Find common ground and use it as a bridge to build rapport. Shared interests create a sense of camaraderie, making it easier to transition from polite small talk to meaningful alliances. Even if you don't share their passions, show curiosity and enthusiasm, it's the fastest way to earn their goodwill.

Step 5: Offer Value Before You Ask

Billionaires are inundated with people asking for favors, so stand out by offering something first. Share an exclusive opportunity, a valuable connection, or even an idea that benefits their ventures. Establish yourself as a peer who adds value to their world. Once you've proven your worth, you can gently pivot to discussing potential collaborations or projects.

Step 6: Play the Long Game

Schmoozing billionaires isn't about instant results—it's about cultivating relationships over time. Stay in their orbit through casual check-ins, sending thoughtful gifts, or inviting them to exclusive gatherings of your own. Consistency builds trust, and trust turns acquaintances into allies. Over time, these relationships will pay dividends in influence, access, and opportunities.

The Billionaire Schmoozer's Creed

Remember, this isn't about friendship, it's about strategy. Every conversation, compliment, and connection is a step toward strengthening your empire. Schmoozing billionaires isn't a skill, it's an art. Master it, and you won't just build relationships; you'll build power.

Hosting Your Own Summit- Climate Talks That Don't Require Sacrificing Comfort

Why attend someone else's summit when you can host your own? As a billionaire, few things reinforce your status more than gathering the world's elite on your terms. A private summit is the ultimate flex, a blend of networking, power projection, and influence consolidation wrapped in a veneer of altruism. And if your summit just happens to discuss global crises like climate change while sparing you any personal inconvenience, well, that's just smart planning. After all, no one said saving the planet had to come at the expense of luxury.

Step 1: The Perfect Venue

The location of your summit sets the tone. Forget sterile conference centers or crowded city hotels, your summit should take place on your private island, aboard your mega-yacht, or in an exclusive mountain resort. The venue isn't just a backdrop; it's a message. It tells attendees that they're in a space where privilege, comfort, and exclusivity reign supreme. Helicopter access, private beaches, and panoramic views are non-negotiables. Your choice of venue should subtly remind everyone that you operate in a different stratosphere, both figuratively and literally.

Step 2: Crafting the Agenda

The agenda is where you showcase your "commitment" to solving global issues, with climate change often taking center stage. But remember, the goal isn't to implement meaningful action, it's to look like you care. Invite panels of carefully selected experts (ideally ones who align with your business interests) to discuss vague but urgent topics such as "Innovative Approaches to Sustainability" or "The Role of Private Sector Leadership in Climate Solutions." Avoid specifics like carbon reduction targets, and focus on lofty goals that sound inspiring but remain safely out of reach. For added flair, schedule a session highlighting your personal contributions to sustainability. A short presentation on your green initiatives, whether it's funding renewable energy research or unveiling your hybrid yacht, will position you as a visionary leader. Bonus points if you manage to tie your philanthropy directly back to your brand.

Step 3: Curating the Guest List

The right attendees elevate your summit from a gathering to an event. Mix fellow billionaires with influential politicians, tech moguls, and a sprinkling of celebrities for good measure. High-profile guests add credibility and media attention, while their attendance ensures the discussions stay suitably high-level and glamorous. Include just activists or academics to provide a sense of balance, but not enough to challenge the tone or call out the contradictions of discussing climate change aboard a gas-guzzling yacht.

Step 4: Luxurious Details That Make an Impact

The details matter. Cater to your guests' every whim with private chefs, personalized itineraries, and world-class entertainment. Gourmet meals sourced from "sustainable" farms and wines from organic vineyards add a performative eco-friendly touch. Every aspect of the summit should exude luxury while incorporating enough greenwashing to deflect criticism. Bamboo utensils, reusable water bottles with your summit's logo, and a promise to plant a forest for every flight your guests take are small gestures that go a long way.

Step 5: The Post-Summit Narrative

The summit's real success isn't in what was discussed, it's in how it's perceived. Hire a PR team to craft glowing press releases highlighting the groundbreaking discussions and your leadership role. Ensure the media frames the event as a crucial step forward in addressing global challenges, with headlines that laud your "visionary commitment" to sustainability. Flood social media with curated photos of attendees sipping cocktails against stunning backdrops, interspersed with quotes about "transformative change." The less concrete action mentioned, the better, this keeps your efforts aspirational and criticism-proof.

The Bottom Line

Hosting your own summit is about consolidating power, projecting influence, and deflecting scrutiny, all while enjoying unparalleled comfort. With the right mix of luxury, optics, and carefully managed narratives, your summit will be remembered not for its outcomes, but for its grandeur. Because in the world of billionaire philanthropy, style always trumps substance.

Navigating Elite Cliques- Building Relationships While Staying on Top

Elite cliques are the billionaire's ultimate arena, a world where power is exchanged over champagne flutes and casual conversations can shape global markets. But make no mistake: these gatherings are battlegrounds in disguise, and merely showing up with a fat wallet won't guarantee your place at the top. The trick is to position yourself as both indispensable and untouchable. First, understand the power dynamics at play. Who commands the room? Who listens, and who is ignored? Observing the unspoken hierarchy allows you to navigate these spaces with precision. Approach the heavy hitters with deference, but always add something to the conversation that showcases your intellect or unique value. At the same time, engage with those lower on the social ladder, it shows magnanimity and creates a loyal buffer of allies eager to sing your praises.

Relationships in these circles are built on calculated exchanges, not emotional connections. To stay on top, you must always bring value to the table, whether it's access to your network, a hot investment tip, or the appearance of camaraderie. But don't be too generous, your influence lies in your exclusivity. Share just enough to build trust while maintaining an air of mystery that keeps people intrigued. At the same time, protect your position fiercely. Elite cliques thrive on competition, and today's ally can quickly become tomorrow's rival. Avoid showing vulnerability, even in casual settings, and subtly undercut anyone who attempts to challenge your dominance. In the end, navigating these circles is a game of power and perception. If you play your cards right, you won't just participate in the clique, you'll define it.

Elite cliques also require careful reputation management. Word travels fast in these circles, so every interaction should reinforce your image as confident, competent, and effortlessly powerful. A single misstep—whether it's an offhand comment or aligning with the wrong person, can shift the social tide against you. Always project grace under pressure, and let rumors of your strategic brilliance precede you. The goal isn't just to build relationships but to cultivate a mystique that ensures others see you as a leader worth following, not just another player in the game.

Chapter 5
Billionaire Burnout and How to Avoid It

Luxury Self-Care- Why Private Islands Are the New Spas

Self-care is essential for anyone, but for billionaires, it's a whole different game. Your wealth and influence aren't just privileges, they're burdens. Endless decisions, public scrutiny, and the relentless pursuit of power can take a toll on even the strongest of moguls. While the average person might escape to a yoga retreat or a spa day, these options simply don't cut it at your level. You need something grander, more exclusive, and utterly impenetrable to the noise of the outside world. Enter the private island: the ultimate sanctuary where you can relax, recharge, and reaffirm your place at the top of the pyramid.

Why a Private Island?

Private islands aren't just about isolation, they're about control. On your island, you're not beholden to anyone. There are no paparazzi lurking in the bushes, no curious tourists ruining the view, and certainly no protestors shouting about wage inequality. Your private island is your domain, where every grain of sand answers to you. Unlike even the most luxurious spas, an island offers a sense of ownership that elevates relaxation to an entirely new level. Here, you don't just visit paradise, you own it. Beyond the practical benefits of solitude, private islands also signal your place in the stratosphere of wealth. They're not just sanctuaries; they're statements. Owning an island tells the world that you've transcended the constraints of landlocked life. It's not just about privacy, it's about declaring, without words, that you've reached a level of success so monumental that you can purchase and command your own piece of the planet.

The beauty of private islands is that they're blank slates, ready to be transformed into the ultimate expressions of your personality and taste. Want a luxury villa with infinity pools overlooking the ocean? Done. Prefer a futuristic eco-lodge to signal your commitment to sustainability? Easy. Your island can be anything you want it to be, a wellness retreat, a high-tech playground, or a mix of both. The point is that every detail is under your control, ensuring that your self-care experience is as unique as you are. Private islands also allow for a level of customization no spa can rival. Bring in the world's best chefs to prepare personalized menus, hire yoga instructors to teach private classes on the beach, or fly in a team of masseuses to cater to your every whim. The entire experience revolves around you, and only you. On your island, the staff's sole mission is to make sure you feel like the king or queen you are.

Wellness Without Compromise

Traditional spas may offer luxury, but they still involve compromise. Even the priciest resorts have other guests, shared spaces, and rules. On a private island, those problems disappear. There's no schedule to follow but your own. No strangers awkwardly sharing a sauna or bumping into you at the juice bar. Your private island is entirely yours, ensuring every moment is tailored to your preferences. Whether you want to spend the day meditating in silence, taking leisurely swims in crystal-clear waters, or hosting a sunset dinner party for a select group of friends, the choice is entirely yours. Self-care at this level isn't about indulgence, it's about restoration. The island becomes a retreat from the pressures of managing vast wealth and influence. It's where you can escape from the expectations placed upon you, free from the constant demands of running an empire. On your island, you can finally take a breath, recalibrate, and focus on what matters most: yourself.

A Playground for the Billionaire Mindset

Of course, a private island isn't just a place to unwind, it's also a playground. The best self-care includes a touch of adventure, and your island can offer it all. From scuba diving in pristine reefs to jet-skiing through turquoise lagoons, every activity reinforces your connection to nature and your mastery over it. Install a state-of-the-art gym overlooking the ocean or a private cinema hidden within the cliffs. Your island isn't just a getaway, it's a reflection of your vision, ambition, and creativity. Private islands offer the perfect setting for discreet networking. Invite select guests to join you for exclusive retreats where deals can be made far from prying eyes. The setting itself signals to your peers that they're not just colleagues, they're part of your inner circle. The relaxed environment of an island creates opportunities for conversations and alliances that would never happen in a corporate boardroom.

Greenwashing Your Paradise

In today's world, even billionaires need to pay lip service to sustainability. Fortunately, private islands offer the perfect stage for performative environmentalism. Power your island with solar energy, plant a "biodiversity sanctuary," and throw in a desalination plant for good measure. These touches allow you to frame your island not just as a retreat, but as a model for eco-friendly living, while conveniently sidestepping the environmental impact of flying guests in on private jets. Don't forget to publicize your efforts. A few well-timed media pieces showcasing your "commitment to the planet" can deflect criticism and bolster your image as a forward-thinking philanthropist.

The Ultimate Escape

Above all, private islands offer an escape like no other. They're not just about what you leave behind, they're about what you gain. A sense of freedom. A space to dream without interruption. A reminder that your success has lifted you to a realm few can ever imagine. In the chaos of modern life, your island stands as a beacon of tranquility, a place where you can retreat, recharge, and reaffirm your power.

Building a Legacy

Finally, private islands aren't just about the present, they're about legacy. Your island isn't just a retreat; it's an heirloom, a piece of the world that will forever bear your name. It's where your family can gather, where future generations will marvel at your foresight and ambition. Naming the island after yourself ensures that long after you're gone, your influence remains, etched into the map and the memory of those who follow. Private islands aren't just the new spas, they're the pinnacle of self-care for the billionaire class. They provide unparalleled privacy, limitless customization, and the perfect backdrop for both relaxation and power moves. Your island isn't just a place to unwind; it's a reflection of your success and a declaration of your dominance. So, billionaire, let the masses have their crowded retreats and their weekend yoga sessions. You deserve more, an island to call your own, where self-care isn't just a practice but a proclamation. Because nothing says "I've made it" quite like owning your very own slice of paradise.

The Emotional Labor of Being Rich- Handling the "Poor Little Rich" Narrative

Being rich is hard, at least, that's the narrative you'll need to perfect if you want to deflect criticism while maintaining your aura of untouchable success. The emotional labor of wealth isn't about actual hardship (let's be honest, private jets and luxury resorts make life pretty sweet); it's about managing how the world perceives you. While the masses might envy your lifestyle, they also resent it. Navigating this delicate balance requires crafting a story of your life that's aspirational yet relatable, privileged yet earned. Enter the "poor little rich" narrative, a powerful tool that allows you to showcase your wealth while disarming critics by highlighting the "burdens" of being fabulously successful.

The key is to acknowledge the downsides of wealth without appearing tone-deaf. Speak about the isolation of extreme success or the pressure to manage vast empires, anything that humanizes you without eliciting outright sympathy. Phrases like, *"It's lonely at the top"* or, *"I'm grateful for my success, but it comes with responsibilities"* are perfect. They remind others of your incredible achievements while framing your life as a challenge, not just a dream. If done well, you'll strike the delicate balance between inspiring envy and muting resentment, turning potential critics into reluctant admirers.

At the same time, don't forget to subtly highlight your contributions. Frame your philanthropy as a source of emotional fulfillment, a way to "give back" despite the pressures of success. Mention the sacrifices you've made for your career or the sleepless nights spent solving big problems (conveniently omitting the teams of people doing most of the work). By carefully managing the "poor little rich" narrative, you don't just deflect criticism, you reinforce your image as a relatable yet aspirational figure. After all, being rich isn't just about having it all, it's about making sure others see the effort it takes to stay on top.

Delegation, Delegation, Delegation- Offload Everything Except Power

Delegation is the lifeblood of the billionaire lifestyle. You don't amass fortunes or empires by doing everything yourself, you do it by offloading every conceivable responsibility to others while keeping a white-knuckled grip on the one thing that truly matters: power. The beauty of delegation isn't just in reducing your workload; it's in ensuring that you remain the unchallenged center of your empire, a sun around which everyone else orbits. Why waste time handling the minutiae of running a company, managing investments, or responding to emails when you can hire a team of experts to handle it all? Delegation isn't a sign of laziness, it's a strategic decision to focus only on the decisions that solidify your position at the top.

The art of delegation begins with identifying what tasks you *shouldn't* be doing. Anything that doesn't directly enhance your power or expand your influence is fair game for offloading. Scheduling meetings? Hire a personal assistant. Managing day-to-day operations? Appoint a trusted CEO. Even philanthropic endeavors can be handed off to a foundation manager who understands how to maintain the illusion of your generosity while keeping you comfortably removed from the details. The goal isn't just to make your life easier, it's to free up your time for the things that matter most, whether that's acquiring new assets, attending exclusive events, or simply enjoying the fruits of your labor in peace. Delegation isn't about shirking responsibility; it's about amplifying your capacity to wield power effectively.

But delegation isn't just about efficiency, it's about plausible deniability. The less you handle personally, the harder it is for anyone to hold you accountable when things go wrong. This is particularly useful in situations where a decision might be controversial or unpopular. By creating layers of decision-makers between yourself and the outcome, you insulate yourself from blame while maintaining ultimate control. If a company you own engages in questionable practices, you can point to the management team as the decision-makers, even if every major move was greenlit by you. Delegation allows you to stay above the fray, a distant and untouchable figure whose hands are clean even when the waters are muddy.

Of course, effective delegation requires the right people. You need a team of loyal, competent individuals who understand their roles and, more importantly, understand that their job is to execute your vision, not question it. This isn't the time for independent thinkers or ambitious upstarts who might challenge your authority. The best delegates are those who thrive on clear directives and have no illusions about where the power truly lies. Reward them well enough to secure their loyalty but keep them dependent on you for their continued success. A delegate who feels indispensable is a threat; one who knows they're replaceable is an asset.

One of the greatest challenges in delegation is maintaining the illusion of involvement. While your delegates handle the grunt work, you must remain the public face of your empire. This means being strategically visible at key moments, an inspiring speech here, a photo-op there, while ensuring that the actual work is being done behind the scenes. This isn't about deception; it's about perception. People want to believe that you're the mastermind behind every success, even if your contribution was little more than signing off on someone else's idea. The ability to balance invisibility with omnipresence is a skill that separates the merely rich from the truly powerful.

Delegation also extends beyond business. Your personal life can, and should, be similarly streamlined. Hire a household manager to oversee your staff, a personal chef to cater to your tastes, and a security team to ensure your safety. Even mundane tasks like booking travel or choosing outfits can be offloaded to experts. This isn't about indulgence, it's about optimizing your life so that every moment is either productive or pleasurable. And creating a life where your time is spent only on the things that truly matter, whether that's closing billion-dollar deals or relaxing on your private yacht.

Ultimately, delegation is the key to maximizing your effectiveness while preserving your sanity. It allows you to focus on the big picture while ensuring that the day-to-day grind is handled by those better suited to it. By offloading everything except power, you create a life where every decision, every action, and every outcome reinforces your position at the top. Delegation isn't just a management technique, it's a philosophy, a way of life that ensures you remain untouchable, unassailable, and in complete control. So, billionaire, delegate with confidence, and remember: the less you do, the more powerful you become.

Living in "Balanced Excess-" How to Hoard Wealth and Enjoy It

The phrase "balanced excess" might sound like an oxymoron, but for a billionaire, it's a way of life. Hoarding wealth and enjoying it are often seen as opposing forces, but with the right mindset, they can coexist beautifully. Balanced excess is the art of indulging in luxury without losing sight of the ultimate goal: keeping as much of your fortune as possible. It's about splurging strategically, where every dollar spent serves a dual purpose, enhancing your lifestyle while reinforcing your power. Whether it's a $200 million mega-yacht or an art collection rivaling a national museum's, your indulgences aren't just pleasures; they're investments in your image and legacy.

The key to balanced excess is understanding that enjoyment doesn't mean letting go, it means leveraging. That private island you bought isn't just a retreat; it's a tax-efficient asset, a networking hub, and a statement piece all rolled into one. The trick is to weave indulgence seamlessly into your wealth preservation strategy. For example, your fleet of private jets might seem like extravagance, but they're also tools of efficiency, allowing you to close deals and expand your empire without the inconvenience of commercial flights. Similarly, your sprawling estates aren't just homes; they're carefully selected trophies of dominance, positioned in tax-friendly jurisdictions and maintained to symbolize your untouchable status. In balanced excess, every luxury has a purpose beyond pleasure, it's a chess move on the board of billionaire life.

This philosophy extends to even the simplest aspects of living. Dining in Michelin-starred restaurants isn't just about the food; it's about occupying spaces where power gathers. Wearing bespoke suits isn't just about style; it's about broadcasting success without needing to say a word. The concept of balanced excess allows you to revel in the spoils of your wealth while ensuring that each indulgence reinforces your dominance. After all, living well isn't just about enjoying your riches, it's about reminding the world that no matter how much you spend, you'll always have more. Balanced excess is the billionaire's sweet spot, where pleasure and power merge into a lifestyle of limitless possibilities.

Chapter 6
How to Handle Bad Press

The Art of the Non-Apology- When "Sorry" Is Just Another Power Move

Apologies are for the weak, or so it might seem. But in the hands of a billionaire, a carefully crafted "sorry" can be a strategic tool for maintaining power, deflecting criticism, and controlling the narrative. The goal isn't to express remorse or admit fault; it's to give the appearance of accountability without conceding anything meaningful. A well-executed non-apology reinforces your authority while silencing critics, ensuring you emerge from any controversy with your reputation intact and your power unchallenged.

The first rule of the non-apology is to never fully accept responsibility. Phrases like, *"I'm sorry if anyone was offended"* or, *"I regret that my actions were misinterpreted"* are classics for a reason. They shift the focus away from your behavior and onto how others perceived it. This subtle blame reversal suggests that the issue isn't what you did but how others reacted, framing you as the victim of overreaction or misunderstanding. The beauty of this approach is that it allows you to acknowledge public outrage without validating it, keeping the focus on your narrative rather than their grievances. Timing and delivery are also crucial. A non-apology should come across as sincere but calculated. Use calm, measured tones and sprinkle in phrases like, *"I take this very seriously"* or, *"I'm committed to learning from this experience."* These statements create the illusion of accountability without requiring you to change anything substantial. Pairing your words with an action that appears proactive, like commissioning a study or donating to a related cause, can further solidify your position. The trick is to ensure the action is symbolic rather than transformative, giving the impression of progress while keeping the status quo firmly in place.

In the end, the non-apology is a masterclass in power dynamics. It lets you dictate the terms of reconciliation while keeping your critics at arm's length. When used effectively, "sorry" isn't a concession—it's a tool to reinforce your control. Because in the world of billionaires, even an apology can be a flex.

Spin It to Win It- Reframing Scandals as Opportunities

For billionaires, scandals are inevitable. Whether it's a lawsuit, a labor controversy, or a tone-deaf comment that sparks outrage, being at the top means living under constant scrutiny. But scandals aren't the end of the world, they're opportunities in disguise. With the right spin, even the most damning incident can be reframed to enhance your reputation, strengthen your brand, or even turn a profit. The key is to seize control of the narrative, transforming public backlash into a story of resilience, reinvention, or misunderstood genius.

The first step in reframing a scandal is swift acknowledgment without outright confession. Timing is critical, address the issue early to prevent the narrative from spiraling out of control. But remember, you're not admitting guilt; you're expressing concern. Use statements like, *"We take these allegations seriously,"* or, *"We are committed to understanding and addressing these issues."* These phrases suggest action without actually admitting to wrongdoing. By framing your response as proactive, you divert attention from the scandal itself to your supposed efforts to "fix" the situation.

Next, identify the emotional core of the scandal and tailor your spin accordingly. If the controversy involves accusations of greed or exploitation, highlight your philanthropic efforts. Emphasize how much you've "given back" to the community, even if the numbers are negligible compared to your wealth. If you're accused of being out of touch, humanize yourself. Share a carefully crafted anecdote about your humble beginnings or a moment of personal struggle that conveniently mirrors the public's concerns. The goal isn't to deny the scandal but to redirect attention to a narrative that portrays you as relatable, misunderstood, or unfairly targeted.

One of the most powerful tools in your arsenal is distraction. While the public focuses on the scandal, unveil a major initiative or make a bold announcement that shifts the conversation. Launch a new product, pledge a hefty donation to a trending cause, or announce a pivot toward a popular movement like sustainability or mental health advocacy. These gestures don't need to solve the problem; they just need to occupy headlines long enough for the outrage to die down. People are easily distracted, and a new, shiny story is often all it takes to make them forget the old one.

Collaboration can also work wonders in reframing scandals. Partner with a trusted figure or organization that aligns with the values you've supposedly violated. If you're accused of environmental harm, collaborate with a conservation group to "develop solutions." If you're called out for unethical labor practices, fund a job training program or appear alongside activists who are "working to make a difference." These partnerships lend credibility to your spin while subtly shifting the focus from your wrongdoing to your newfound commitment to change.

Social media is another powerful tool for reframing scandals. Use your platforms to control the narrative directly, engaging with followers to show that you're "listening" and "learning." Share images of you volunteering, meeting with experts, or looking contemplative in front of a whiteboard. The visuals alone can sway public perception, even if the substance behind them is thin. Social media also allows you to amplify the voices of supporters, whether they're employees defending your character or fans praising your "authenticity." Publicly thanking these individuals creates an echo chamber of positivity around your brand.

At the heart of reframing a scandal is reframing yourself. Scandals present a chance to rewrite your identity in the public eye. You're not just a billionaire caught in a controversy; you're a visionary leader navigating challenges, a philanthropist addressing systemic issues, or a trailblazer unfairly targeted for being ahead of your time. Use the scandal as a launchpad to introduce a "new chapter" in your life or career. Frame it as a turning point, even if nothing substantive changes behind the scenes. The narrative of growth and evolution is irresistible to the public, especially when paired with polished PR and just enough action to lend it credibility.

Lastly, lean into the inevitability of outrage fatigue. Scandals burn hot but rarely for long. By staying calm, controlling the story, and focusing on long-term reputation management, you can outlast the public's anger. Over time, even the most egregious scandals are forgotten, or at least overshadowed by the next outrage to capture attention. The key is to weather the storm without overreacting, giving the public just enough to satisfy their desire for accountability without compromising your position.

The Role of Controlled Outrage- Why Owning Media Pays Off

For billionaires, public opinion is both a weapon and a shield, and controlling the narrative is essential to maintaining power. Enter the media, your ultimate tool for shaping perceptions, managing outrage, and ensuring that even the harshest criticisms work to your advantage. Owning media outlets, or at least heavily influencing them, isn't just a luxury, it's a strategic necessity. With the right approach, you can transform public scrutiny into controlled outrage, a force you can manipulate to reinforce your dominance while deflecting meaningful challenges to your wealth and power.

The Art of Setting the Agenda

Owning or influencing media outlets allows you to set the agenda for public discourse. You control what gets attention, how issues are framed, and, perhaps most importantly, what is conveniently ignored. Scandals that could damage your reputation can be downplayed, reframed, or buried entirely, while favorable narratives about your philanthropy, innovation, or leadership take center stage. When the media you own or fund becomes the primary source of information for the public, your version of events becomes the dominant reality.

Consider a hypothetical labor dispute in one of your companies. Without media influence, the story might focus on unfair wages, worker protests, and your staggering wealth. With media influence, however, the narrative shifts. Instead of workers' grievances, headlines might highlight your company's "commitment to economic growth" or "plans for future job creation." By shaping the conversation, you don't just control the message, you control the public's perception of who you are.

Outrage as a Distraction

Controlled outrage is one of the most powerful tools in your arsenal. Outrage is inevitable, people will always find reasons to criticize billionaires, but it can be managed and even redirected. When you own or influence media, you can amplify controversies that distract from your own shortcomings. Is the public angry about your tax avoidance? Shift the focus to an inflammatory comment made by a celebrity or a divisive social issue. Outrage burns bright but brief; by giving the public a new target, you ensure their attention moves away from you.

Additionally, controlled outrage can be weaponized to discredit your critics. If activists, politicians, or journalists challenge your practices, the media you control can frame them as extremists, hypocrites, or self-serving opportunists. By casting doubt on their motives, you shift the focus away from their arguments and back onto their credibility. Even if their criticisms are valid, the public's attention will be split, reducing the impact of their claims.

Creating a Hero Narrative

Owning media also allows you to cultivate a hero narrative for yourself. While others face unfiltered scrutiny, you can use your platforms to present yourself as a visionary, philanthropist, or problem-solver. Controlled outrage plays a role here, too, it provides opportunities for you to swoop in and appear magnanimous. If there's public outrage over a societal issue, your media can frame your actions as part of the solution, whether it's a donation, a speech, or a symbolic gesture. The key is ensuring that your narrative dominates the discussion, overshadowing any doubts about your motives.

For example, if there's public anger over climate change and your company's environmental record is questionable, your media can focus on your "commitment to sustainability." Articles, op-eds, and glowing profiles can highlight your investments in renewable energy or a "green initiative" launched by your foundation, deflecting criticism while reinforcing your image as a forward-thinking leader.

Managing Outrage Cycles

One of the most overlooked benefits of media influence is the ability to control the outrage cycle. Outrage, by nature, is short-lived, but the timing of its rise and fall can be critical. By strategically releasing stories, amplifying certain narratives, or introducing new controversies, you can control the rhythm of public anger. If a scandal involving you is gaining traction, your media can release a sensational story about an unrelated topic, ensuring that your issue fades into the background. Conversely, if you want to distract from a competitor's success or a regulatory threat, you can stir up outrage that dominates the news cycle, leaving no room for competing narratives.

The Subtlety of Influence

Direct ownership of media outlets isn't always necessary; influence can be just as powerful. Funding think tanks, supporting journalists, or owning stakes in digital platforms allows you to guide narratives without appearing heavy-handed. Subtlety is key—your involvement should be just distant enough to maintain the illusion of neutrality. For example, a journalist working for a media outlet partially funded by your foundation might not realize how their coverage aligns with your interests, but the outcome is the same: stories that reinforce your narrative while minimizing dissent.

Shaping Public Priorities

Media influence also allows you to shape what the public cares about. By highlighting certain issues and ignoring others, you guide societal priorities in ways that benefit you. For instance, if public pressure for higher taxes on billionaires is gaining momentum, your media can amplify stories about "wasteful government spending" or the dangers of overregulation. The public's focus shifts from your wealth to broader systemic issues, diluting the push for reforms that might impact you directly.

Conversely, you can use media to champion causes that align with your business interests. If your investments lean toward renewable energy, your outlets can emphasize the urgency of climate action, positioning you as both a hero and a savvy investor. If you own data-driven companies, stories about the benefits of innovation and technological advancement can subtly push public sentiment in favor of policies that protect your interests.

Reinforcing Power Structures

Ultimately, media influence reinforces the power structures that allow you to thrive. By shaping public discourse, you ensure that the system remains favorable to you while appearing impartial. The narrative becomes less about what's fair and more about what's possible, with you cast as the inevitable leader of progress. The media's role here isn't just to protect you, it's to normalize your dominance, ensuring that challenges to your power are seen as disruptive rather than necessary.

The Ethical Shield

Ironically, owning media also provides an ethical shield. Critics may accuse you of hoarding wealth or exploiting workers, but your media can highlight your charitable contributions, thought leadership, and "visionary" projects. The same outlets that might otherwise criticize you become platforms for showcasing your "values," effectively neutralizing dissent. Public outrage is deflected or reframed, ensuring that even your worst missteps are cast as minor imperfections in an otherwise admirable legacy.

Conclusion

Owning or influencing media isn't just about avoiding bad press, it's about controlling the narrative in every sense. With the right strategy, you can turn scandals into opportunities, shift public priorities, and reinforce your position as an untouchable figure of influence. The role of controlled outrage in this process cannot be overstated, it's the fuel that keeps the media machine running, allowing you to guide the public's emotions while staying firmly above the fray. For a billionaire, media influence isn't just a convenience, it's a cornerstone of power.

Making Public Outrage Fade Quickly- A Guide to Distraction Tactics

Public outrage is a billionaire's persistent nemesis. It flares up unpredictably, fueled by scandal, inequality, or the latest viral exposé of your wealth-hoarding ways. Left unchecked, outrage can escalate into public demands for accountability, government investigations, or even the dreaded regulation. But here's the good news: outrage burns hot, but it rarely burns long, if you know how to manage it. The key is not to extinguish the fire outright but to redirect its heat elsewhere, leaving you unscathed. With the right distraction tactics, you can make public fury dissipate faster than a PR crisis manager can say "unprecedented commitment to change."

Step 1: Control the Narrative with Immediate Action

The moment outrage begins to build, you need to take control of the narrative. This doesn't mean admitting guilt or fixing the underlying issue—it means taking symbolic action that shifts attention to your supposed effort to address the problem. Announce a "comprehensive review" of your practices or pledge a significant-sounding donation to a related cause. The point isn't to solve anything but to signal that you're "listening" and "taking steps." Words like *"commitment," "collaboration,"* and *"solution-focused"* work wonders here.

For example, if outrage flares up over poor working conditions in your factories, you might pledge to "enhance workplace safety" with a multi-million-dollar initiative. The actual funds can trickle out over years, or never, but the immediate announcement creates a headline that suggests you care. By steering the conversation toward your "proactive response," you redirect attention from the issue itself to your supposed efforts to resolve it.

Step 2: Amplify a New Story

People have short attention spans, and a new story, especially one with emotional weight or sensational drama, can quickly eclipse their outrage. Use your media connections to amplify a distracting headline. It doesn't even need to be related to the original scandal. A celebrity controversy, a natural disaster, or even a flashy new product launch can serve as the perfect diversion.

If your personal scandal is dominating the news, consider orchestrating or capitalizing on a "feel-good" story. For instance, sponsor an event that highlights your company's philanthropic work, like providing scholarships to underprivileged students or hosting a high-profile charity gala. Make sure your name is front and center, ensuring that any coverage shifts from criticism to admiration.

Step 3: Deflect Blame to Broader Systems

When outrage targets you specifically, widen the scope of the discussion. Shift the blame from yourself to the system at large, reframing the issue as a complex societal challenge rather than a personal failing. For instance, if you're accused of tax avoidance, highlight the flaws in the tax code and position yourself as a supporter of "comprehensive reform." Statements like, *"The system needs fixing, and I'm committed to being part of the solution,"* shift the focus from your actions to abstract problems that no one expects you to solve overnight.

This tactic works especially well when paired with symbolic gestures, such as funding think tanks or joining panels that discuss solutions. The goal is to appear as an ally in addressing the issue, even if you're doing nothing substantive. By broadening the conversation, you dilute the focus on your individual role and redirect outrage toward impersonal, systemic challenges.

Step 4: Shift Focus to a Tangential Scandal

If the heat is still on you, divert attention to another controversy that might seem related but doesn't directly implicate you. This works especially well if you can nudge public discourse toward your critics or competitors. For instance, highlight another company's ethical lapses or point to societal issues that make your own scandal seem minor by comparison.

Subtly frame the narrative to suggest that while your actions may not have been perfect, others are far worse. Leak a report, fund a study, or amplify a news story that directs public attention elsewhere. By focusing outrage on a bigger or tangential target, you reduce scrutiny on yourself.

Step 5: Use Time to Your Advantage

Outrage has an expiration date, and one of the simplest ways to handle it is to wait it out. By offering just enough distractions and symbolic gestures to keep the worst of the backlash at bay, you allow public anger to dissipate naturally. Over time, the outrage will be overshadowed by the next controversy, the next viral moment, or the public's general fatigue.

While you wait, maintain a low profile. Avoid unnecessary public appearances or statements that could reignite the issue. At the same time, keep your PR machine running in the background, quietly releasing positive stories about your business ventures, philanthropy, or leadership. These narratives don't need to address the scandal directly, they just need to provide alternative stories for people to latch onto.

Step 6: Partner with Strategic Allies

When public outrage threatens your reputation, align yourself with trusted institutions or figures to bolster your image. Partnering with well-regarded charities, thought leaders, or community organizations allows you to borrow their credibility. These alliances serve as shields, deflecting criticism and reinforcing your role as a "force for good."

For example, if your company is accused of environmental harm, collaborate with a conservation group to launch a green initiative. Highlight the partnership through media coverage, ensuring that the focus shifts from your misdeeds to your "commitment" to sustainability. The more your allies vouch for you, the harder it becomes for critics to sustain their outrage.

Step 7: Control the Emotional Tone

Outrage thrives on emotion, so defuse it by striking a calm, empathetic tone in your responses. Acknowledge people's concerns without validating their anger. Statements like, *"I understand why people feel this way, and I'm committed to making things better,"* neutralize the emotional intensity of the backlash. Pair this with visible displays of humility, appear at community events, release photos of yourself engaged in reflective moments, or share stories of personal growth. The goal is to project calm leadership while subtly suggesting that the outrage is exaggerated.

Conclusion

Public outrage is a storm that can be weathered with the right distractions, deflections, and displays of strategic humility. The goal isn't to confront or resolve the outrage head-on but to redirect its energy until it fades. By controlling the narrative, amplifying alternative stories, and positioning yourself as part of the solution rather than the problem, you can turn even the fiercest backlash into a fleeting memory. Outrage is temporary, your wealth and power, however, are not. Play your cards right, and you'll emerge not only unscathed but perhaps even stronger than before.

Chapter 7
Offloading Responsibility, Without Losing Control

Blame as a Strategy- How to Protect Yourself by Throwing Others Under the Bus

Blame, when wielded correctly, is one of the most effective tools in a billionaire's arsenal. In a world where public scrutiny is relentless, and accountability is always looming, knowing how to shift blame away from yourself and onto others is an essential skill. It's not about being heartless, it's about being strategic. The goal isn't just to escape consequences but to ensure your power and reputation remain intact while someone else takes the fall. Mastering the art of blame is less about outright deceit and more about reframing narratives, choosing the right scapegoats, and ensuring the story always positions you as the misunderstood visionary trying to navigate a flawed world.

The Foundations of Blame-Shifting

Throwing someone under the bus begins with understanding the nature of power hierarchies. In any system, there are layers of responsibility, and your job is to ensure you remain insulated from direct accountability. This starts with delegation. The more layers of management, consultants, or intermediaries between you and the decision-making process, the easier it is to deflect blame when something goes wrong. When controversy arises, you're not the one who approved the policy or made the call, you're the leader who "trusted the wrong people." This allows you to frame yourself as the ultimate victim of poor advice or execution.

It's also essential to maintain plausible deniability. This doesn't mean you're unaware of what's happening, it means ensuring there's no concrete trail tying you to questionable actions. When you delegate authority, ensure directives are vague enough that the blame can't easily trace back to you but clear enough that the task gets done. Ambiguity is your ally. If push comes to shove, you can always claim your instructions were "misinterpreted" or "taken out of context."

Choosing the Right Scapegoat

The effectiveness of blame depends heavily on the scapegoat you select. Ideally, this should be someone who is expendable in the grand scheme of your operations. Mid-level managers, PR teams, or external consultants make excellent targets. They're close enough to the situation to appear responsible but far enough down the hierarchy that their downfall doesn't destabilize your position.

The scapegoat should also have a plausible connection to the controversy. If a labor dispute arises, it's the operations manager who failed to implement your "commitment to workplace safety." If a scandal breaks regarding environmental harm, it's the head of sustainability who "misrepresented the company's efforts." The more credible the connection, the easier it is to shift focus away from yourself and onto them.

However, don't rely solely on individuals. Sometimes, abstract entities make the best scapegoats. Blame "market forces," outdated regulations, or even society at large. By pointing to systemic issues, you position yourself as a problem-solver rather than a perpetrator. Statements like, *"This is a challenge faced by the entire industry,"* or, *"We are committed to working within a flawed system to drive change,"* shift the spotlight from your actions to broader, impersonal problems.

Framing Yourself as the Hero

The art of blame-shifting isn't just about deflecting criticism, it's about reframing yourself as a leader trying to navigate a messy world. When the public sees you as someone taking responsibility for fixing issues, even if you caused them, they're more likely to forgive past mistakes. The key is to act swiftly and decisively. Fire the scapegoat, announce a new initiative, and position yourself as the one taking bold action to "right the wrongs."

Language matters here. Use phrases like, *"I take full responsibility for ensuring this doesn't happen again,"* or, *"While I was not aware of the details, I recognize that the ultimate accountability rests with me."* These statements sound like admissions of guilt but are carefully designed to deflect actual blame. They suggest you're stepping in to clean up someone else's mess, reinforcing the narrative that you're a proactive and responsible leader.

Media Management and Public Perception

Media plays a crucial role in how blame is assigned. Controlling the narrative through owned or influenced outlets ensures the story is framed in your favor. Issue press releases that emphasize the corrective actions you're taking, highlighting your "commitment to transparency" and "willingness to learn." Simultaneously, use your PR team to quietly downplay the involvement of top executives, yourself included, while pushing stories about the scapegoat's failings.

Social media offers another opportunity to shape perception. Carefully curated posts can show you meeting with affected parties, engaging with experts, or reflecting on "lessons learned." The goal is to flood the conversation with positive or neutral narratives, drowning out criticism and shifting focus to your efforts to move forward. If the scapegoat is a visible figure, ensure their role in the controversy is subtly but firmly established in public discussions.

When to Throw Someone Under the Bus Publicly

Timing is everything. Throwing someone under the bus too early can make you appear ruthless, while waiting too long risks letting the scandal escalate beyond your control. Ideally, the scapegoat should be sacrificed once public pressure reaches its peak but before irreversible damage is done to your reputation.

The act itself should be decisive but framed as reluctant. Statements like, *"It's with a heavy heart that we part ways with [Scapegoat's Name],"* or, *"We appreciate their service but recognize that new leadership is necessary to move forward,"* allow you to appear fair and thoughtful rather than opportunistic. The public loves accountability, and a well-timed dismissal satisfies their demand for consequences without jeopardizing your position.

Internal Management: Keeping the Team in Line

While blame-shifting can protect you externally, it can create tension internally. No one likes to see their colleagues, or themselves, thrown under the bus. To maintain morale, it's essential to manage your team carefully. Frame the scapegoat's departure as a necessary sacrifice for the greater good, emphasizing that the company's survival depends on difficult decisions. Reward those who remain loyal with promotions, bonuses, or public praise to reassure them of their security.

Privately, however, make it clear that loyalty is non-negotiable. The scapegoat's downfall should serve as a cautionary tale: dissent or failure to shield you from scrutiny will not be tolerated. By maintaining a balance of rewards and consequences, you can ensure your team remains compliant and motivated, even in the face of public backlash.

Mitigating Long-Term Risks

While blame-shifting is an effective short-term strategy, it can create long-term risks if mishandled. Overusing scapegoats or throwing the wrong people under the bus can lead to public cynicism or internal instability. To mitigate these risks, diversify your tactics. Pair blame-shifting with proactive measures like preemptive philanthropy, public displays of humility, or bold new initiatives that overshadow past controversies.

Additionally, consider rotating the scapegoats. If the same department or individuals are always blamed, it can raise suspicions. Spread the accountability across different areas of your operations, ensuring no single narrative takes root. This prevents any pattern from emerging and keeps critics guessing.

The Ethics of Blame-Shifting

Let's be honest: ethics are secondary to survival in the billionaire world. However, maintaining a veneer of integrity is crucial. Blame-shifting isn't about outright deception, it's about managing perceptions in a way that protects your ability to continue driving change, innovation, or, let's face it, profit. The public expects leaders to take responsibility, but they're also remarkably forgiving when those leaders show a willingness to "correct" mistakes. By shifting blame strategically, you're not just protecting yourself, you're ensuring the stability of the empire you've built.

Conclusion: Blame as a Necessary Evil and a Damning Reflection

Blame, when skillfully wielded, is undeniably effective. It safeguards reputations, preserves power, and keeps empires intact. But let's not sugarcoat it: the art of throwing someone under the bus isn't just about strategy, it's about ruthlessness. To use blame as a tool is to acknowledge the darker side of leadership, where the end always justifies the means, and where personal survival trumps loyalty, fairness, or even morality. If you've made it this far, billionaire, you might already know that this isn't just a guide, it's a mirror. And what you see reflected back might not be flattering.

Because let's face it: throwing others under the bus, no matter how elegantly done, is fundamentally an act of betrayal. It's choosing self-preservation over accountability, deflection over growth, and convenience over integrity. Every carefully worded press release, every scapegoat sacrificed to the public's demand for justice, and every orchestrated narrative serves to reinforce the same message: *My wealth, my power, and my legacy matter more than the lives affected by my decisions.* Sure, you can dress it up in corporate jargon or spin it as a necessary act of leadership, but deep down, you know the truth.

And yet, the world you inhabit almost demands this kind of behavior. Being a billionaire means operating in a world where public scrutiny is constant, where every decision is dissected, and where outrage is always one viral tweet away. In this reality, blame-shifting isn't just a tactic, it's a lifeline. You can't afford to stumble. The stakes are too high, the margins too thin, and the expectations too unforgiving. But does necessity excuse the cost? Is it truly worth sacrificing relationships, trust, and perhaps a part of your humanity to ensure you remain untouchable?

Think about the people you've thrown under the bus, or will throw in the future. They might not be saints, but they're human beings, often with far less power than you. Mid-level managers, consultants, department heads, these are people with families, mortgages, and dreams of their own. Sacrificing them to the gods of public opinion may save your skin, but it wrecks theirs. And for what? To shield someone who already has more money than they could spend in ten lifetimes? To protect an empire that could withstand the loss of a few million without even flinching?
Worse yet, employing these strategies perpetuates the very system of

inequality that fuels public outrage in the first place. Each time blame is shifted, a scapegoat takes the fall, and the structure of power remains untouched. The public demands accountability, but instead, they get the illusion of justice, an individual punished while the machine chugs along, unchanged. It's a cycle that ensures those at the top stay there, while those at the bottom continue to absorb the consequences of decisions they didn't make. It's efficient, yes. But is it ethical? Is it humane?

Of course, you could argue that this is just the cost of leadership, that tough decisions come with the territory, and that survival, both yours and your empire's, requires a certain level of detachment. But don't fool yourself into thinking this is admirable. It's expedient, yes, but it's also cowardly. True leadership involves owning your mistakes, facing criticism head-on, and, occasionally, making sacrifices that hurt your bottom line for the sake of doing what's right. If you're unwilling to do that, then perhaps your power isn't as secure as you think it is.

So, billionaire, before you prepare your next scapegoat, take a moment to ask yourself what kind of leader you want to be. Will you be remembered as someone who rose above the fray, accepting accountability and using your influence to create meaningful change? Or will you be just another untouchable figure, hoarding wealth and power while leaving a trail of discarded lives in your wake?

Blame may be a powerful strategy, but it comes with a cost, not just to others, but to yourself. Use it sparingly, and only if you're willing to confront the uncomfortable truth of what it says about you. Because in the end, the measure of your legacy won't be in the fortunes you've hoarded but in the people you've spared from the wheels of your bus.

The "Invisible Hand" Excuse- Letting the System Take the Blame

The "invisible hand" of the market is one of the most useful myths ever perpetuated, particularly for billionaires. It's the ultimate deflection tool, a way to offload responsibility for the inequities and harm caused by your actions, or inaction, onto a nebulous, uncontrollable force. When you invoke the invisible hand, you absolve yourself of blame while elevating your wealth and power as proof that you're merely playing by the rules of an inevitable and impartial system. After all, if the market decided you deserve billions, who are you to question its wisdom? The invisible hand isn't just an excuse; it's a shield that protects your empire from criticism, regulation, and reform.

Blame the Game, Not the Player

The beauty of the invisible hand excuse lies in its ability to reframe the narrative. When critics point out the exploitative practices that built your fortune, whether it's underpaid workers, environmental destruction, or tax avoidance, you can respond with a shrug and a well-rehearsed line about how "the market operates." It's not your fault that wages are low; it's the natural result of supply and demand. You didn't choose to offshore your manufacturing; the market dictated it. Every decision you make, no matter how harmful, can be justified as adherence to the impartial forces of economics.

This excuse isn't just convincing to the public, it's comforting to you. By invoking the invisible hand, you can silence any lingering doubts about the morality of your actions. You're not hoarding wealth; you're allocating resources efficiently. You're not exploiting workers; you're responding to market signals. The invisible hand allows you to reframe greed as rationality, exploitation as inevitability, and self-interest as altruism.

The Market as an Amoral Arbiter

One of the most insidious aspects of the invisible hand excuse is its ability to present the market as an amoral, apolitical force. This framing is crucial because it strips away the human element of decision-making, reducing complex systems to simple equations. When you defer to the market, you're not just absolving yourself of blame, you're reinforcing the idea that no one is truly responsible. This creates a convenient vacuum where accountability disappears, and the public is left to accept inequality, poverty, and environmental degradation as natural phenomena, not the result of deliberate choices made by people like you.

By leaning into the narrative of the market's neutrality, you also shield yourself from reform. If the market is amoral, then any attempt to regulate it becomes an emotional overreach, a misguided effort to impose morality where it doesn't belong. You can frame calls for higher wages, stricter environmental protections, or fairer tax policies as dangerous interventions that disrupt the "natural order." This isn't just an argument, it's a weaponized ideology that ensures your wealth and power remain intact while critics are dismissed as naïve idealists.

Leveraging Economic Literacy (or the Lack Thereof)

The invisible hand excuse thrives on the public's limited understanding of economics. Most people don't know, or care, that the idea of the invisible hand originated as a metaphor, not a literal mechanism. You can exploit this lack of literacy by presenting yourself as a humble servant of the market, someone who simply follows its dictates. By using jargon like "market efficiencies," "resource allocation," and "global competitiveness," you can dazzle critics into submission while avoiding any meaningful conversation about the morality of your actions.

When faced with outrage, double down on the technicalities. Argue that the complexities of the global economy are beyond the grasp of the average person and insist that you're simply making the "tough decisions" required to keep the system functioning. This approach doesn't just deflect blame, it positions you as a steward of economic stability, a role that demands respect and deference.

Individualism Over Systems Thinking

The invisible hand excuse also thrives on the cultural emphasis on individualism. By focusing on your personal success story, you can distract from the systemic issues that enabled your wealth. Frame your achievements as the result of hard work, innovation, and risk-taking, conveniently omitting the societal structures that supported your rise. For instance, if you benefited from tax breaks, government subsidies, or inherited wealth, downplay these factors and highlight your "entrepreneurial spirit."

This individualist narrative serves two purposes. First, it reinforces the idea that you're not to blame for inequality because you "earned" your success. Second, it discourages systemic critiques by framing inequality as a personal failing rather than a structural issue. If someone isn't thriving, it's not because the system is broken, it's because they didn't work hard enough. This rhetoric shifts the blame away from you and onto the very people who suffer most from the system you exploit.

The Hypocrisy of "Free Markets"

While the invisible hand excuse relies on the idea of free markets, the reality is that billionaires rarely operate in truly free markets. Behind every great fortune is a web of government policies, corporate lobbying, and monopolistic practices that tilt the playing field in your favor. Yet, the invisible hand allows you to obscure these realities, presenting yourself as a champion of competition rather than a beneficiary of systemic advantages.

When faced with criticism, you can invoke the language of free markets to defend practices that are anything but. If someone challenges your monopoly, argue that you've simply "outcompeted" rivals. If questioned about tax avoidance, insist that you're following the law and that the real problem lies with legislators. This rhetorical sleight of hand allows you to defend your actions while deflecting responsibility onto faceless institutions.

Weaponizing Public Cynicism

Public cynicism about institutions is another powerful ally in the invisible hand excuse. By framing the market as inevitable and apolitical, you tap into the public's mistrust of government and bureaucracy. Present yourself as someone who succeeds despite government interference, not because of it. This positioning allows you to shift blame onto regulators, policymakers, and activists who "don't understand" the market's complexities.

When criticism mounts, weaponize this cynicism further by painting reform efforts as overreach. Argue that higher taxes will stifle innovation, that regulations will hurt small businesses (even if they won't touch yours), and that wealth redistribution is an attack on "freedom." This rhetoric turns public opinion against those advocating for change, ensuring that the system remains as favorable to you as ever.

The Moral Cover of "Efficiency"

Efficiency is one of the invisible hand's most powerful justifications. By framing your actions as efforts to maximize efficiency, you can sidestep moral questions entirely. Whether it's laying off workers, automating processes, or cutting corners on environmental protections, you can argue that these decisions are necessary to maintain competitiveness. Efficiency becomes a moral good in itself, overriding concerns about fairness, sustainability, or human impact.

This argument works particularly well when paired with economic inevitability. If layoffs are framed as the result of market forces, not greed, you're no longer the villain, you're the reluctant decision-maker doing what's necessary to keep the company afloat. Efficiency absolves you of blame while shifting focus to abstract metrics like profit margins or shareholder value, making it easier to justify actions that harm people or the planet.

Rebranding Exploitation as Progress

The beauty of the invisible hand excuse is its ability to transform even the most blatant exploitation into a story of progress. It allows you to frame your actions, no matter how harmful, as necessary steps toward a brighter future. Polluting rivers? That's not environmental destruction, it's the cost of economic development and job creation. Automating industries and laying off thousands of workers? That's not heartless profiteering, it's innovation, paving the way for a more efficient and technologically advanced society. By leaning into the narrative of progress, you shift the conversation from what's being lost to what could be gained, ensuring that any criticism of your practices seems shortsighted or even regressive.

This strategy works particularly well when paired with the rhetoric of inevitability. Position your actions as simply part of the march of progress, driven by market forces beyond anyone's control. Emphasize the benefits to society, no matter how abstract or delayed they might be. For instance, you can claim that automating a workforce will lead to long-term economic growth or that offshoring production allows consumers to enjoy lower prices. Never mind that the immediate consequences, job losses, community collapse, or environmental degradation, are devastating. The promise of a utopian future is often enough to placate critics or, at the very least, confuse the argument.

Moreover, rebranding exploitation as progress turns critics into enemies of advancement. Activists who challenge your practices are no longer fighting for fairness or sustainability, they're obstacles to innovation, stuck in the past while you lead the charge toward the future. By controlling the narrative, you position yourself as the visionary, a pioneer sacrificing short-term comfort for long-term gain. It's not just a defense, it's a masterstroke, reframing your exploitation as essential to society's evolution.

The Legacy of the Invisible Hand

The invisible hand excuse isn't just a rhetorical strategy, it's a foundational ideology that protects billionaires from accountability while ensuring the system remains rigged in their favor. By deferring responsibility to the market, you reinforce the myth that wealth inequality, environmental harm, and systemic exploitation are inevitable rather than deliberate. This narrative doesn't just benefit you, it perpetuates a system that ensures the rich stay rich while everyone else struggles to survive.

But let's not pretend this excuse comes without cost. Every time the invisible hand is invoked to deflect blame, it erodes trust in institutions, deepens inequality, and reinforces the public's sense of powerlessness. It's a convenient shield, but one that leaves a trail of disillusionment and injustice in its wake.

As a billionaire, you might find comfort in the invisible hand's absolution. But remember: the more you rely on this excuse, the more you expose the fragility of the system that protects you. Because in the end, even the most carefully constructed myths can crumble under the weight of their own contradictions. And when they do, no excuse—not even the invisible hand—will be strong enough to hold back the tide of accountability.

Sacrificial Lambs- Why Fall Guys are Essential

In the high-stakes world of extreme wealth and unrelenting power, the concept of the "fall guy" isn't just a useful tool, it's an essential component of maintaining the billionaire ecosystem. Sacrificial lambs, or the people and entities strategically placed to absorb blame, are the unsung heroes of empire-building. These individuals and scapegoats protect the delicate image of billionaires as untouchable visionaries, ensuring that their gilded towers remain pristine while the inevitable muck of human failure sticks to someone else. Without fall guys, how could billionaires possibly navigate the treacherous waters of public scrutiny, political criticism, and the occasional environmental or labor disaster? The answer is simple: they couldn't. Fall guys are as integral to modern capitalism as profits themselves, and honestly, who wouldn't want to be part of such a noble, sacrifice-rich tradition?

Let's dispense with the illusion of morality right away. Sacrificial lambs aren't just acceptable in this system—they're necessary. After all, someone has to bear the brunt of public outrage when a billion-dollar initiative goes wrong or when layoffs devastate an entire community. If not the billionaire, whose brilliance and drive surely transcend such mundane concerns as accountability—then who? Critics might cry foul, pointing out the inherent unfairness of one person taking the fall for decisions orchestrated by a wealthy few. But that's just naive whining. This isn't about fairness, it's about survival. The survival of the individual billionaire, of the empire they built, and, let's be honest, of the very system that allows them to hoard obscene wealth while billions of others scrape by. Sacrificial lambs are the grease on the wheels of capitalism, and the machine doesn't move without them.

When a fall guy is chosen, it's rarely accidental. A good sacrificial lamb is handpicked, someone perfectly positioned to absorb the fallout while preserving the integrity of the billionaire's brand. Perhaps it's a middle manager whose role is just high-profile enough to be credible as the source of a scandal but not high enough to actually matter to the company's operations. Or maybe it's an external contractor or a subsidiary conveniently labeled as "rogue" when their actions attract unwanted attention. These choices are calculated, ensuring that the lamb's sacrifice is both believable and effective. And who better to take the fall than someone already benefiting from their proximity to power? After all, these individuals knew the risks when they signed up to work for a titan of industry, didn't they?

Of course, the system itself makes fall guys not only practical but inevitable. The modern corporation is designed as a labyrinth of responsibility, with layers upon layers of management and decision-making designed to obscure who is truly in charge. When something goes wrong, blame can cascade down this structure like water through a sieve, pooling around the most convenient figure. And here's the beauty of it: no one ever questions the system itself. Instead, the focus remains squarely on the individual deemed responsible, sparing the billionaire from having to sully their hands with the messiness of accountability.

Let's not forget the masterful PR work that accompanies these sacrifices. When a scandal breaks, the billionaire steps forward, not to accept blame, of course, but to express their deep disappointment and unwavering commitment to fixing the problem. They might announce the resignation of the fall guy, paired with a rousing statement about their company's dedication to "doing better." Perhaps they'll even pledge a vague sum of money to a related cause, ensuring that the headlines shift from the wrongdoing to their supposed acts of contrition. The fall guy is gone, the billionaire looks like a hero, and the public, appeased by the ritual, moves on. It's a win-win, well, except for the sacrificial lamb, but let's not dwell on that.

Now, let's address the elephant in the room: the supposed ethical problem with all of this. Is it wrong to let someone else take the blame for decisions you made or endorsed? Is it cruel to scapegoat an individual to protect your image and empire? Absolutely not, if you frame it correctly. In the grand scheme of things, what's one ruined career compared to the preservation of a system that supposedly benefits everyone? After all, billionaires are job creators, innovators, and philanthropists. If they fall, doesn't everyone else suffer, too? By shielding themselves from accountability, they're not just protecting their wealth, they're safeguarding the very fabric of society. Or at least, that's the story they tell, and as long as it holds, who's to argue?

But let's not stop there. Sacrificial lambs don't just protect billionaires—they also serve a vital societal function. They provide the public with a sense of closure, a symbolic act of justice that allows us all to move on without questioning the deeper issues at play. The fall guy is the lightning rod for our collective outrage, a figure upon whom we can heap our dissatisfaction with corruption, inequality, and unchecked greed. In doing so, we avoid the uncomfortable truth: that the system isn't broken—it's working exactly as intended. Sacrificial lambs distract us from this realization, ensuring that the real culprits remain safely in the shadows.

And yet, it's impossible to ignore the toll this cycle takes. By perpetuating a system that relies on scapegoats, we allow the actual problems, concentrated power, systemic inequality, environmental collapse, to fester unchecked. The fall guys change, but the underlying dynamics remain the same, dragging us deeper into a morass of distrust and dysfunction. Every time a sacrificial lamb is offered up, we tacitly agree to let the system off the hook, ensuring that the same mistakes, the same abuses, will happen again. It's a cycle of decay masquerading as progress, and the more we buy into it, the harder it becomes to imagine a different way.

So, let's not pretend that sacrificial lambs are a benign necessity. They are a symptom of a system that values optics over substance, survival over accountability, and profit over people. And while billionaires may argue that these sacrifices are for the greater good, the reality is that they're nothing more than a convenient way to maintain the status quo. The world may continue to turn, but it does so on the backs of those deemed expendable, their lives and reputations ground into dust so that the rich and powerful can keep their hands clean.

In the end, the real tragedy isn't the fate of the sacrificial lambs, it's the fact that we, as a society, have accepted this arrangement as normal. We've been sold the idea that accountability is a luxury, that the powerful must be protected at all costs, and that individual sacrifice is a small price to pay for the preservation of wealth and order. But as the cracks in this system grow wider, as inequality deepens and trust erodes, it becomes increasingly clear that the cost of these sacrifices is far higher than we've been led to believe. And unless we find the courage to question the foundations of this system, we'll all remain lambs to the slaughter, one way or another.

He Was Just the Coffee Guy

An example rant if you get caught being associated with a bad guy

"Look, I don't know who that guy is. I never met him. Someone said he worked here, but honestly, I couldn't tell you what he did. Coffee? Maybe. I think someone mentioned he was in logistics, but does it really matter? The point is, he's not me, and that's all anyone really needs to know. When a situation goes south, like that "unfortunate miscommunication" with the labor strike or that tiny oversight with environmental compliance, you need someone, anyone, to step forward, even if they were just the coffee guy.

It's not personal. It's business. Sure, it might seem unfair to hang the entire mess on a low-level employee, but let's not act like it's all bad for them. A public firing can really put someone on the map, you know? Their name's in the headlines for the first time ever! Sure, it's next to words like *"gross negligence"* or *"scandal,"* but fame is fame. Maybe someone else will hire them out of pity. "Oh, that's the guy who ruined everything? Let's give him a second chance!" People love a good redemption arc.

The truth is, I can't be expected to keep track of everyone who works here. Do you know how many people it takes to run an empire? Thousands. Tens of thousands. Am I supposed to remember every name, every face, every job description? It's not like I personally hired the guy. He could've been an intern for all I know. Maybe he just wandered in off the street one day, carrying a clipboard to look official. Happens all the time.

So, yeah, I don't know who he is. But if blaming him keeps the headlines off me, then he was absolutely the one who dropped the ball. After all, someone's got to take the fall, and it's definitely not going to be me."

Chapter 8
How to Identify with the Working Class

"Relatable Billionaire" Personas- How to Shop at Walmart for the Cameras

Ah, the relatable billionaire, a modern myth crafted with the precision of a luxury timepiece and sold to the masses as proof that wealth hasn't distanced you *too* far from the everyday struggles of ordinary people. In an age where public opinion can be as fickle as stock prices, appearing relatable isn't just good optics, it's survival. And what better way to cement your down-to-earth image than by strolling the fluorescent-lit aisles of Walmart, putting discounted laundry detergent into your cart for all the world to see? Shopping at Walmart is not about bargains; it's about branding. Done right, it's a masterclass in public relations. Done poorly, it's a meme waiting to happen.

Step One: Set the Scene

First things first: make it look spontaneous, even though it absolutely isn't. Relatable billionaire outings are never spur-of-the-moment; they're meticulously choreographed events designed to create an illusion of authenticity. Call ahead to ensure the store manager is aware of your visit but emphasize that it must appear casual. No special treatment, no red carpets, unless, of course, that "regular shopper" vibe needs some polishing. Brief your security team to stay just out of frame but close enough to whisk you away if the public gets too enthusiastic. The goal is to project an image of approachable wealth, not chaos.

Dress the part, but don't overdo it. A crisp white button-down, jeans (preferably brand-new and tailored to within an inch of their lives), and sneakers that look "well-loved" but cost more than the average monthly rent will do nicely. You want to look like someone who *could* afford to buy the entire store but chooses not to. The watch, if visible, should be understated but expensive enough to remind people you're not *really* one of them.

Step Two: Curate the Cart

The contents of your shopping cart are critical. They tell a story. This isn't the time to stock up on imported truffle oil or that $300 artisanal kombucha you secretly love. Instead, opt for items that scream "I'm just like you." Think bulk paper towels, store-brand cleaning supplies, and family-sized cereal boxes. Bonus points if you toss in a pack of socks or a modest kitchen gadget like a toaster. The more mundane, the better.

Avoid indulgences that break the illusion. No one will believe you eat frozen pizza or budget-brand peanut butter, so don't insult their intelligence. A few aspirational items, say, organic almond milk or a name-brand coffee, are fine, but the balance must lean toward the ordinary. If you have children, this is the perfect opportunity to grab a toy or two "for the grandkids." Even if it's purely performative, the image of a billionaire caring about a $9 action figure warms hearts and fills comment sections with praise.

Step Three: Work the Room

Once inside, engage with the environment like a true Walmart regular, or at least your version of one. Wander purposefully but casually. Pause to examine price tags, squinting thoughtfully, as if budgeting is a real concern for you. Maybe strike up a friendly conversation with an employee about a product's quality or availability. If you're feeling particularly daring, complain about inflation, it's a surefire way to win sympathy and make headlines. The key is to appear genuinely engaged without looking rehearsed. Smile warmly at fellow shoppers, and if someone recognizes you, embrace the moment. Take selfies, shake hands, and listen to their stories with a nod of feigned interest. Every interaction is a potential soundbite that humanizes you.

Avoid rookie mistakes like appearing lost or out of place. No billionaire who's been properly briefed should gape at self-checkout kiosks like they're alien technology. Practice beforehand if necessary. Fumbling with the card reader or asking "What's a rollback?" will ruin the illusion faster than a leaked offshore account.

Step Four: The Exit Strategy

The checkout process is your grand finale. Politely refuse offers to skip the line, and for the love of PR, don't whip out a black card. Cash or a modest credit card will suffice, something relatable like a basic Visa or Mastercard. Small talk with the cashier is mandatory. Ask how their day is going, empathize with their workload, and maybe even drop a line about how much you "love this store." If they ask, "Do you want a bag for that?" hesitate for a beat, as if you're seriously considering the nickel charge, before graciously agreeing. This is your moment to shine as a "normal" person.

As you leave, carry at least one bag yourself. Letting an assistant handle everything while you walk ahead empty-handed destroys the narrative. Bonus points if you comment to a reporter or a shopper on your way out: *"You know, it's been years since I had time to do this, what a great store!"* Authenticity is an illusion, and this is your closing act.

Why It Matters

The relatable billionaire persona isn't just a PR stunt; it's a strategic defense mechanism. In a world increasingly critical of wealth inequality, appearing relatable diffuses resentment. When the public sees you buying the same products they do, it reinforces the myth that success hasn't changed you, that deep down, you're still one of them. It's a calculated move to protect your brand, your fortune, and, ultimately, the system that made you rich in the first place.

Critics might call this pandering, but isn't that the point? Appearing relatable isn't about actually connecting with people; it's about giving them just enough to believe they could be you someday. It perpetuates the dream that anyone, if they work hard enough, can achieve the impossible. Never mind that the deck is stacked, the game rigged, and the ladder missing half its rungs. If you can shop at Walmart with a smile, so can they, right? And if they believe it, they'll defend you against the critics, the regulators, and the protesters. They'll call you a "self-made hero," a "role model," and a "real American success story."

The Risks

Of course, this persona is not without its pitfalls. Any misstep can backfire spectacularly. A poorly staged visit risks turning you into a meme or, worse, a symbol of tone-deaf elitism. Consider the billionaire who bought a $7 lamp from Walmart and bragged about it as if they'd just discovered fire. The internet skewered them, not for their purchase, but for the audacity of pretending that saving $3 on a lamp was relatable when their annual yacht maintenance costs more than most people's lifetime earnings.

To avoid such disasters, always do your homework. Know the environment, anticipate potential pitfalls, and never underestimate the public's ability to spot insincerity. Authenticity may be an illusion, but it's one that requires meticulous upkeep.

Conclusion

Shopping at Walmart for the cameras isn't about the shopping—it's about the story. It's about crafting an image of yourself as approachable, grounded, and empathetic, even if your reality is anything but. It's a tool to deflect criticism, humanize your wealth, and perpetuate the fantasy that anyone can achieve what you have. Done well, it's a masterstroke of public relations. Done poorly, it's a cautionary tale. Either way, it's proof that in the world of billionaires, even the simplest act, buying paper towels, can be transformed into a spectacle of calculated relatability. Because in the end, it's not about what's in your cart; it's about what's in the public's mind.

The Myth of the Self-Made Billionaire- Rewriting your origin story

The myth of the self-made billionaire is one of the most enduring narratives in modern society, a rags-to-riches tale crafted to inspire admiration, loyalty, and, most importantly, an untouchable image of moral superiority. It's a story so powerful that it convinces millions of people that your success was entirely the result of grit, genius, and determination, ignoring the structural advantages, generational wealth, systemic inequalities, and outright exploitation that paved the way for your ascent. Rewriting your origin story isn't just about crafting a compelling narrative; it's about ensuring that no one looks too closely at the inconvenient truths. This isn't a lie, it's branding. A billionaire without a self-made story is like a castle without walls, vulnerable to the hordes of critics demanding accountability, redistribution, or even basic fairness. By positioning yourself as the plucky underdog who climbed the mountain against all odds, you not only secure public admiration but also ensure that anyone questioning your wealth is dismissed as bitter, lazy, or simply jealous.

The first step in rewriting your origin story is to focus on struggle, whether it's real, exaggerated, or entirely fabricated. Even if you grew up in a mansion with a trust fund and a private chauffeur, there's always some detail that can be reframed to suggest hardship. Maybe your parents instilled a strong work ethic, forcing you to mow the sprawling estate lawn. Or perhaps you worked a summer job "just like everyone else," conveniently omitting that it was at a company owned by your family. These anecdotes don't need to withstand scrutiny; they just need to create the illusion of relatability. The goal is to emphasize your perseverance while downplaying the safety nets and shortcuts that made your journey significantly easier than the average person's. Success isn't enough, you need to sell the idea that you *earned* it.

Next, shift the focus to your "vision." The self-made myth relies heavily on the perception that you saw potential where others saw nothing. If your wealth came from exploiting labor or leveraging connections, frame it as foresight. You didn't inherit opportunity—you *created* it. Were you born into a family with industry ties? No, you were a "scrappy entrepreneur" who "learned the ropes" by "watching your parents hustle." Did you have access to elite education and mentors? No, you "sought out knowledge" and "built a network through sheer determination." The key is to make every advantage sound like a personal achievement. Rewriting your origin story isn't about denying privilege, it's about recasting it as a series of hurdles you overcame with extraordinary ingenuity.

The narrative must also highlight risk-taking, even if the risks were minimal. The self-made billionaire myth thrives on the idea that you gambled everything and won. Perhaps you "bet on yourself" by starting a company, carefully omitting the fact that you were backed by venture capitalists or a generous family loan. Maybe you "slept on a couch in your early days," but leave out that the couch was in a luxury apartment. These details humanize you while maintaining the illusion of struggle. Even if your risks were calculated and your safety net was secure, the story should make it sound like you were teetering on the edge of ruin. People don't admire wealth, they admire the illusion of bravery it represents.

Of course, no origin story is complete without a nemesis. Every hero needs an obstacle, whether it's an indifferent marketplace, skeptical peers, or the abstract villain of "society's expectations." By positioning yourself as someone who defied convention, you cast your wealth as a triumph over adversity rather than a consequence of systemic exploitation. Did you revolutionize an industry? Emphasize how everyone doubted you. Did you build a company by underpaying workers or skirting regulations? Frame it as a bold move to "challenge outdated norms." The goal is to recast criticism as envy and controversy as evidence of your trailblazing spirit.

One of the most important aspects of the self-made myth is the strategic omission of inconvenient details. Perhaps you benefited from government contracts, tax breaks, or regulatory loopholes—these are not part of the story. If your wealth is tied to questionable practices, like environmental destruction or labor exploitation, those details are irrelevant to the narrative you're crafting. The self-made billionaire myth isn't about accuracy; it's about perception. People don't want to hear about the compromises and shortcuts, they want to believe in the magic of meritocracy. By carefully editing your story, you give them exactly what they want.

This myth isn't just about inspiring admiration; it's also a powerful defense mechanism. If you're self-made, then criticism of your wealth becomes an attack on hard work itself. Anyone advocating for higher taxes, stronger regulations, or wealth redistribution can be dismissed as anti-ambition or anti-success. By embodying the myth of the self-made billionaire, you position yourself as a symbol of possibility, a walking advertisement for the idea that anyone can achieve greatness. Never mind that the system you operate within is designed to concentrate wealth at the top, your story convinces people that their lack of success is a personal failing, not a systemic issue. In this way, the myth protects not just you but the entire structure of inequality that enables your wealth.

The self-made narrative also serves to distance you from other billionaires. By emphasizing your unique journey, you create the illusion that your success is fundamentally different from that of your peers. This isolates you from criticisms aimed at "the billionaire class" and reinforces the idea that your wealth is deserved while others' might not be. You're not just another rich person, you're a visionary, a disruptor, a hero. This differentiation is crucial for maintaining your public image, particularly in an era when skepticism of wealth is growing. By framing yourself as an exception, you protect yourself from the broader critiques of capitalism.

The myth, of course, isn't without its contradictions. You must constantly walk the line between relatability and exclusivity. If you lean too heavily into the "everyman" narrative, you risk losing the aura of exceptionalism that justifies your wealth. Conversely, if you emphasize your genius too much, you alienate the very people you're trying to relate to. The trick is to maintain the illusion of accessibility without ever becoming truly accessible. You're a billionaire, after all, the idea that anyone could actually relate to your life is absurd. But as long as they believe they *could*, the myth remains intact.

And what of the societal consequences of perpetuating this myth? The self-made billionaire narrative doesn't just distort your story, it distorts reality itself. By focusing on individual success, it diverts attention from the systemic factors that create and sustain inequality. It teaches people to idolize wealth rather than question it, to see billionaires as solutions rather than symptoms of a broken system. In doing so, it reinforces the status quo, ensuring that the cycle of exploitation, concentration, and exclusion continues unchecked. But this, too, is part of the myth's power. By rewriting your origin story, you don't just protect yourself, you protect the very system that allowed you to rise.

Performative Humility- Looking down-to-earth while living in a penthouse

If wealth is power, then humility is the charm that makes it tolerable. For billionaires, performative humility is not just a personality trait—it's a carefully cultivated defense mechanism. The art of appearing down-to-earth while residing in a penthouse or owning a fleet of private jets is a skill that few master, but those who do reap the rewards of public admiration and reduced scrutiny. It's not about actually being humble; it's about looking humble in a way that reassures the public and keeps critics at bay. Performative humility is a spectacle, a tightly choreographed performance designed to make wealth feel less threatening. Done well, it allows you to have it all—the riches, the power, the accolades, without the pesky resentment or guilt that might otherwise come with it.

The key to performative humility lies in contradiction. Your wealth should be obvious, but your demeanor should suggest you're indifferent to it. You're not flaunting your penthouse lifestyle; you're just "living modestly" in an 8,000-square-foot space with panoramic city views. Your private jet isn't a status symbol, it's a tool to "maximize productivity" or "reduce carbon emissions" (even if you have no idea how that works). Performative humility is about acknowledging your privilege just enough to defuse resentment while subtly reinforcing how deserving you are of it. It's a balancing act, a sleight of hand that turns opulence into relatability.

Highlighting your Roots Real or Imagined

The first rule of performative humility is to highlight your roots, real or fictional. It doesn't matter if you were born into a life of luxury; what matters is the story you tell. Dig deep into your family history for any trace of struggle, no matter how tenuous. Perhaps your great-grandparents were immigrants who "worked hard to give the family a better life." Maybe you had a part-time job in high school or "learned the value of a dollar" from a strict parent who made you pay for your own first car (which, incidentally, was likely far nicer than most people's second or third cars). The point isn't accuracy, it's relatability. The more you can humanize your origins, the easier it becomes to mask the vast gulf between your life and the lives of those you aim to impress.

An Air of Nonchalance

Next, develop a persona of casual indifference toward wealth. People don't hate billionaires because they're rich; they hate billionaires who seem obsessed with being rich. By downplaying your interest in material possessions, you can disarm critics while maintaining your opulent lifestyle. Wear understated clothing, think plain but perfectly tailored, and avoid logos or ostentatious displays. Drive a practical car to certain public appearances, even if a chauffeured Rolls-Royce is waiting nearby. If anyone asks about your penthouse, dismiss it as "a place to sleep," even if it's decked out with custom art installations and a personal chef. The goal is to project an air of simplicity that reassures people you're not the kind of billionaire who lets money define them, even as it quietly shapes every aspect of your existence.

Out in the Open, Turn on the Charm

Public displays of humility are another cornerstone of the performance. Philanthropy is an obvious and effective tool here. Donate to high-visibility causes, but always do so in a way that feels personal and modest. Don't just write a check; make a show of being "hands-on." Attend fundraisers and talk about how "humbled" you are by the work being done. Use phrases like *"I'm just doing my part"* or *"It's a privilege to give back"* to shift the focus away from the scale of your wealth and onto the supposed purity of your intentions. If you can, choose causes that align with your public persona. If you're a tech billionaire, support STEM education. If you're in real estate, fund housing initiatives. The key is to create a narrative that ties your success to broader social good, even if the impact of your giving is negligible compared to the wealth you hoard.

Never be *Offline*

Social media is another powerful tool for performative humility. Use it to share glimpses of your "ordinary" life, a candid photo of you eating a burger, a selfie in a hoodie, or a tweet about how you still feel awkward at parties. These carefully curated moments create an illusion of accessibility that distracts from the reality of your privilege. The trick is to look relatable without ever actually being relatable. Posting about how you "splurge on a $4 coffee" is safe; posting about your $40,000 private island getaway is not. By sharing just enough to seem grounded, you can maintain the illusion that you're not so different from the average person.

Platitudes are Your Friend

Another critical component of performative humility is the strategic acknowledgment of privilege. You don't need to admit how your wealth was really built, whether through generational advantage, exploitation, or outright luck, but you should nod to the idea that you've had some help along the way. This acknowledgment should always be vague, emphasizing general concepts like *"standing on the shoulders of giants"* or *"the importance of teamwork."* These statements signal humility without ever implicating you in the systemic inequalities that sustain your wealth. It's a way of saying *"I'm lucky"* without anyone asking why your luck seems to come at the expense of others.

Fake Gratitude is your Friend

Performative humility also involves cultivating a sense of gratitude. Publicly thank your team, your mentors, or even society at large for their role in your success. Gratitude shifts the focus away from you and onto the people or circumstances you claim to credit. This tactic not only makes you appear humble but also insulates you from criticism. After all, how can someone attack you when you've already positioned yourself as endlessly thankful? Gratitude is a preemptive strike against resentment, a way of disarming critics before they even take aim.

Sometimes Less is More

However, performative humility isn't just about what you do, it's about what you don't do. Avoid overt displays of wealth that might undermine your narrative. No one wants to see their "relatable billionaire" wearing a diamond-encrusted watch or flaunting a $500,000 car collection. Even if you own these things (and let's be honest, you do), keep them out of sight. Excessive displays of wealth are bad for the brand, and in the age of social media, it only takes one poorly timed Instagram post to ruin years of carefully crafted humility.

Know Your Audience

Despite its effectiveness, performative humility has its limits. It works best on an audience that wants to believe in the myth of the good billionaire, the generous capitalist who uses their wealth for the greater good. But in a world where inequality is increasingly impossible to ignore, this act can start to feel hollow. When your penthouse lifestyle is juxtaposed against homelessness, or your private jet is criticized in the context of climate change, even the best performance can ring false. The cracks in the façade grow wider with every headline, and the illusion of humility becomes harder to sustain.

Always be On

Yet, even as the public grows more skeptical, performative humility remains a vital tool for billionaires who wish to protect their wealth and power. It's not about solving the problems your wealth represents, it's about distracting from them. As long as people are focused on your *appearance* of humility, they're less likely to question the systems that allowed you to amass so much wealth in the first place. The performance is a smokescreen, a way to keep the conversation on your character rather than your complicity.

But of Course

In the end, performative humility isn't really about being humble, it's about control. It's about controlling how people see you, what they think of you, and whether they view your wealth as a problem to be solved or a success to be celebrated. It's a dance, a balancing act between opulence and relatability that requires constant maintenance but yields extraordinary results. Because as long as people believe you're one of the "good ones," they'll forgive you for living in that penthouse. Or at least, they'll let you keep it.

Tales of Struggle- Borrowing hardships to humanize yourself

The most compelling tales of struggle often spring not from the lived experiences of billionaires but from a willingness to borrow, distort, or outright steal the hardships of others. For the ultra-wealthy, creating a narrative of adversity isn't just about entertainment, it's about survival. Society increasingly demands authenticity from its icons, and what's more authentic than a good old-fashioned tale of overcoming the odds? Of course, when your biggest obstacle in life was deciding between which luxury boarding school to attend, the odds aren't exactly in your favor. That's where imagination, a complete lack of scruples, and an inflated sense of self-importance come into play. You don't have to live a hard life to sell a hard-luck story. You just have to be shameless enough to make one up—and if you're a billionaire, shamelessness is practically a prerequisite.

The art of stealing hardships begins with knowing your audience. People want to believe that success is earned, not inherited. They need to see their heroes as reflections of themselves, gritty, determined, and triumphant against all odds. But here's the rub: most billionaires' lives couldn't be further from this narrative. Their stories are built on inherited wealth, generational advantage, or the exploitation of others. None of that sells books, inspires admiration, or staves off the pitchforks. So, the solution is simple: pilfer a hardship or two. Don't just borrow; embellish. Turn your private school's strict dress code into a tale of financial struggle. Recite tales of bootstrapping from the comfort of a chair upholstered in cashmere. The key isn't accuracy, it's relatability. As long as it feels true, no one will bother to check if it actually is.

Of course, some might argue that fabricating struggle is morally reprehensible. And sure, they'd be right, but who cares? Billionaires live in a world where morality is negotiable, a PR asset to be deployed when useful and discarded when inconvenient. What's a little theft of narrative in the grand scheme of things? After all, if people believe your made-up hardships, they'll be less likely to scrutinize the very real harm you've caused. Maybe you crushed a union or dumped pollutants into a river, but hey, you once "went hungry" for a day in college because you spent your allowance too quickly. You understand struggle! And if people buy that story, they'll defend you to the bitter end.

The best struggles to steal are those that resonate universally. Poverty is a favorite because it's easy to manipulate and difficult to disprove. Start with vague anecdotes: *"We didn't have much growing up,"* you might say, leaving out that "not much" meant only having one vacation home instead of three. Or go bolder: *"My family lived paycheck to paycheck,"* conveniently ignoring that those paychecks came from lucrative board memberships and investment portfolios. The beauty of these tales is their malleability. They don't need to withstand scrutiny; they just need to evoke sympathy. Sprinkle in details like sharing a bedroom with a sibling (in your 8,000-square-foot mansion) or eating simple meals (cooked by the live-in chef). Authenticity is optional; relatability is mandatory.

If poverty doesn't suit your brand, consider stealing someone else's identity as a scrappy underdog. Did you grow up in a well-connected family that provided every opportunity? No problem. Frame yourself as the black sheep who "made it on your own." Maybe your family helped finance your first business, but you can twist that into a tale of relentless hard work. *"I had to fight to prove myself,"* you'll say, conveniently omitting the safety net that cushioned every stumble. Turn nepotism into rebellion, privilege into adversity. It's all about reframing the facts to make yourself look like a self-made hero.

For the more daring among the billionaire set, outright theft of another person's story can be particularly effective. If someone in your orbit, a friend, a colleague, a distant cousin, has lived a genuinely challenging life, appropriate their struggle as your own. Change a few details, add a personal flair, and voilà: their hardship becomes your ticket to public adoration. Maybe your assistant once struggled with homelessness, or your housekeeper worked multiple jobs to support their family. Take their pain, polish it up, and make it part of your mythos. Sure, it's exploitative, but when has that ever stopped you? You're not in the business of fairness; you're in the business of winning hearts and minds.

Fabricating struggle isn't just about building sympathy, it's about control. A well-crafted hardship narrative shifts the focus away from the ways you've exploited others or manipulated the system. Instead of asking why you pay workers starvation wages or evade taxes, the public marvels at how far you've come. They see your wealth as proof of perseverance, not exploitation. It's the perfect distraction, a sleight of hand that keeps people too enchanted by your story to notice the damage you've caused.

Of course, stealing hardship isn't without risks. Every so often, someone will dig too deep, uncovering the discrepancies in your tale. Perhaps they find out that your "humble beginnings" were anything but or that your rags-to-riches story conveniently skips over the part where you were handed a fortune on a silver platter. When this happens, your best defense is to double down. Insist that your struggle was "emotional" or "spiritual," even if it wasn't financial. Say things like, *"Success isn't just about money—it's about overcoming the odds within yourself."* Shift the narrative to something intangible and unprovable. If all else fails, accuse your critics of being cynical or jealous. People want to believe in the myth of the self-made billionaire, and as long as you give them a reason to, they'll ignore the cracks in your story.

What makes stealing hardship particularly insidious is how it erases the experiences of those who actually live through struggle. When billionaires co-opt tales of adversity, they diminish the voices of people who endure real hardship. It's an act of theft, not just of narrative but of credibility. Yet this is precisely why it's so effective. By positioning yourself as someone who has "been there," you disarm criticism from those who truly have. Who are they to challenge you, when you've suffered too? It's a grotesque inversion of reality, one that ensures the people most affected by inequality remain marginalized while you bask in their stolen spotlight.

Does this make you a terrible person? Absolutely. But does it matter? Not really. Billionaires don't rise to the top by caring about the moral implications of their actions. If you've already trampled workers, manipulated markets, and evaded accountability, what's a little narrative theft on top of that? It's just another tool in your arsenal, another way to maintain your grip on power. You're not here to win awards for ethics; you're here to win, period.

In the end, the real tragedy isn't that billionaires steal hardships, it's that society lets them. We want so desperately to believe in the myth of the self-made success story that we ignore the glaring contradictions and the harm caused by these fabrications. We allow billionaires to rewrite their histories because their lies comfort us, providing hope that we too might one day overcome impossible odds. It's a collective delusion, one that props up the very systems that keep most people struggling while a select few thrive.

Stealing hardship isn't just about crafting a compelling story, it's about perpetuating a lie that keeps the world as it is. And for the billionaire willing to abandon any pretense of morality, it's an invaluable tool. So go ahead: borrow, embellish, or outright fabricate. Take the struggles of others and make them your own. After all, if no one stops you, why would you ever stop yourself?

While we are Talking about you Being an Awful Person

The Definitive Billionaire Awfulness Scale

Let's face it: being a billionaire isn't inherently a neutral state, it's a spectrum of awfulness. Accumulating such obscene wealth in a world rife with inequality, hunger, and suffering already places you on shaky moral ground. But how far you tilt into the realm of cartoonish villainy depends on how flagrantly you embrace your billionairedom. Below is a scale to help you determine just how awful a billionaire you truly are. Spoiler alert: If you're reading this, the needle is already leaning toward *pretty awful*.

1-2: The Benevolent Mirage

You're that mythical unicorn of billionaires, someone who *seems* less awful because you've mastered the art of looking generous without actually giving up much. Sure, you donate a fraction of your wealth to charity, but let's be real: even if you gave away $100 million, it's pocket change compared to your net worth. You constantly talk about "giving back" but only to causes that align with your brand. Your philanthropy is a tax write-off wrapped in a press release. At least you're trying to distract everyone from the systemic inequality you represent, which, on this scale, puts you on the low end of awfulness. For now.

3-4: The Greenwasher Extraordinaire

You've decided to lean into sustainability, not because you care about the planet, but because it's great **PR**. Your companies market "eco-friendly" products while quietly dumping pollutants into the environment. You offset the guilt of your private jet use by planting a forest somewhere (probably a tax haven), then post about it on social media with hashtags like #DoingMyPart. You probably have a solar panel or two on your 12,000-square-foot mansion but conveniently ignore that your lavish lifestyle consumes the resources of a small city. At this level, you're actively misleading people into thinking you're saving the world while continuing to profit from its destruction. Awful, but still in a polished suit.

5-6: The Exploiter-in-Chief

You don't even bother pretending anymore. Your business empire is built on the backs of underpaid workers, many of whom can't afford the products they create. You've lobbied against minimum wage increases and union efforts while publicizing your *"commitment to workforce development."* Layoffs? Outsourcing? Cutting corners on safety? All in a day's work. Your profits always take precedence, even if it means entire communities collapse under the weight of your greed. You're starting to shed that faux-benevolence mask, and it's getting harder to feign surprise when people hate you.

7-8: The Gaslighting Mogul

This is where you fully embrace your role as an unapologetic gaslighter. You tell workers that *"we're all part of a family"* while slashing benefits. You argue that your obscene wealth is actually good for society, claiming it inspires innovation and creates jobs, even though most of your wealth is hoarded or parked in offshore accounts. When people criticize you, you paint yourself as the victim of "anti-success bias." Your talking points are lifted straight from Ayn Rand, and you genuinely believe the world should be grateful to have you in it. At this point, you're not just awful, you're exhausting.

9-10: The Gilded Tyrant

Congratulations, you've ascended to the top tier of billionaire awfulness. You actively use your wealth to manipulate governments, crush dissent, and silence critics. You fund politicians to ensure the laws work in your favor, lobby for tax breaks while hoarding enough wealth to feed entire nations, and wage PR campaigns to smear anyone who challenges you. You've probably bought a social media platform, not to improve it, but to amplify your ego and stifle opposing views. Your name is synonymous with greed, and your legacy is a testament to the idea that no amount of wealth is ever enough. You're not just awful, you're the blueprint for systemic collapse.

11+: The Supervillain

At this stage, you've gone full Bond villain. You live in a private fortress, surrounded by literal walls, metaphorical walls, and probably a moat. You're developing an escape plan for when society collapses (a collapse you've likely contributed to), complete with underground bunkers and spaceships. You've crossed into outright nihilism, fully aware of the harm you're causing but too insulated to care. The world burns while you build bigger yachts, and your only concern is that people are rude about it on Twitter. You're not just awful, you're a cautionary tale. And yet, you sleep soundly at night on a mattress stuffed with money.

Where Do You Fall?

The scale isn't linear, it's logarithmic. Each level exponentially increases your awfulness, with the greatest leaps occurring when you stop even pretending to care about anything beyond yourself. Wherever you land, the key takeaway is this: being a billionaire in a world where millions lack basic necessities is inherently awful. The only question is how much you embrace that awfulness, and how much damage you're willing to do in the process.

Chapter 9
Love in the Time of Power

Pre-Nups and NDAs- Why love needs legal protection

For billionaires, love is a battlefield, one fraught with potential legal landmines, power imbalances, and the ever-looming specter of betrayal. In a world where every relationship could devolve into a PR disaster or a financial liability, pre-nuptial agreements (pre-nups) and non-disclosure agreements (NDAs) are less about romance and more about self-preservation. These legal tools aren't just insurance policies, they're shields against vulnerability, designed to protect wealth, reputation, and power at any cost. Of course, by the time you're drafting a document to safeguard against the fallout of your own love life, you're probably already losing the plot. But hey, when you've got billions at stake, why let something as trivial as human connection derail your empire?

Pre-nups are the cornerstone of billionaire relationship management. These agreements ensure that no matter how messy a breakup gets, your fortune remains intact. A pre-nup doesn't just define who gets what in the event of divorce; it sets the tone for the entire relationship. From day one, it establishes that love may be grand, but it's no match for financial pragmatism. Assets acquired before marriage are meticulously accounted for, as are those accrued during the relationship. Investments, properties, businesses, and intellectual property are all locked down tighter than the vault at Fort Knox. Some agreements even include lifestyle clauses, stipulations about behavior, fidelity, and privacy, because what says *"I trust you"* more than legally binding rules for how to behave as a partner?

Then there's the NDA, a document so ubiquitous in billionaire circles it might as well be part of the wedding vows. *"Do you promise to honor, cherish, and never disclose sensitive information to the press?"* An NDA ensures that your secrets—whether personal, professional, or downright scandalous—remain buried forever. It's not enough to safeguard wealth; reputation must also be preserved. NDAs cover everything from intimate details of the relationship to business dealings discussed over breakfast. Signatures are often required before the first date, ensuring that even the potential for a casual fling doesn't result in a tabloid exposé.

But here's the thing: when your relationships require an army of lawyers to function, you've already lost something far more valuable than money. Love, that messy, unpredictable, infuriatingly human emotion, isn't supposed to be transactional. Yet for billionaires, it's reduced to a series of contractual obligations, a risk to be mitigated rather than a bond to be cherished. You've built a fortress around your heart and bank account, ensuring that no one can truly touch you—emotionally or financially. It's efficient, sure, but it's also profoundly sad.

Imagine the conversations that lead to these agreements. *"Honey, I love you, but let's talk about what happens if we split and you try to take half my fortune."* Romantic, isn't it? A pre-nup is essentially a declaration that even in the throes of passion, you're thinking about an exit strategy. It's the ultimate acknowledgment that you don't trust love to last, or worse, that you don't trust the person you're supposedly in love with. And while you might justify it as protecting yourself from gold-diggers or opportunists, what you're really protecting yourself from is vulnerability. Billionaires don't get to be billionaires by letting people see their soft underbelly. But the irony is that by shielding yourself so completely, you ensure that no one ever gets close enough to love you for who you are, rather than what you're worth.

Of course, you tell yourself it doesn't matter. Who needs emotional intimacy when you have yachts, private islands, and a team of advisors to validate your every decision? Love is messy, unpredictable, and frankly, inefficient. Wealth, on the other hand, is orderly, calculable, and reliable, as long as you've lawyered up. You convince yourself that these legal protections are a necessary evil, that they're simply the cost of living in a world where everyone wants a piece of you. But deep down, you know the truth: you've traded something real for the illusion of control, and no amount of money can buy it back.

And yet, this is the world we live in, a world where relationships are commodities, love is a liability, and the idea of trust is laughable. Billionaires epitomize this emptiness, their lives a grotesque display of opulence devoid of meaning. They're not building relationships; they're drafting agreements. They're not finding partners; they're vetting potential co-signers. It's a transactional existence, one that reduces even the most profound human connection to a series of clauses and conditions.

But who cares, right? You're rich. Isn't that all that matters? In a time defined by obscene wealth and shallow values, the ability to protect yourself from the messy realities of human connection is seen as a virtue. You don't need love, you've got power. You don't need intimacy, you've got influence. And when you die alone in your gold-plated penthouse, surrounded by legal documents that preserved your fortune but cost you your humanity, at least you'll know you played the game well. Bravo.

Yet, even as you sign your pre-nups and enforce your NDAs, there's a part of you that wonders if it's all worth it. Not the part you let anyone see, of course. On the surface, you're the picture of confidence, a titan of industry who has everything figured out. But late at night, in the rare moments when the noise of your empire quiets, you might feel the faintest pang of something resembling regret. You've built walls so high no one can climb them, and now you're alone in the fortress. The NDAs, the pre-nups, the endless legal protections—they've kept you safe, but at what cost?

In the end, the tragedy of the billionaire isn't their wealth, it's their emptiness. They've turned love into a transaction, relationships into liabilities, and life into a series of carefully managed risks. And the saddest part? They'll never admit it. They'll keep signing contracts, enforcing clauses, and pretending that their wealth makes them immune to the human condition. But all the money in the world can't fill the void they've created. And no legal document, no matter how airtight, can protect them from themselves.

Romantic Strategies for Wealth Preservation- Choosing a Spouse Who Won't Get "Ideas"

Romance, for billionaires, is rarely a matter of the heart; it's a matter of strategy. While the masses can afford to follow their feelings, those perched atop mountains of wealth must approach relationships like mergers, carefully assessing risks and rewards before signing on the dotted line. After all, love can be unpredictable, and unpredictability is the enemy of wealth preservation. A poorly chosen partner, someone with inconvenient notions about fairness or independence, can spell disaster. To avoid such pitfalls, it's essential to choose a spouse who won't get "ideas," especially the kind that involve challenging your control over your fortune or, heaven forbid, expecting equality in the relationship.

Step One: Recognize the Threat

Let's be clear: marriage, for the ultra-wealthy, is a double-edged sword. On one hand, it offers stability, companionship, and, in some cases, the chance to build an aesthetically pleasing brand of shared success. On the other, it introduces risk, both financial and reputational. A spouse who decides they want a bigger slice of the pie can set off a chain reaction of legal battles, tabloid scandals, and, worst of all, the potential erosion of your net worth. Romantic entanglements are inherently risky, and mitigating those risks is the cornerstone of any billionaire's relationship strategy.

The primary threat is a partner who begins with love but eventually develops inconvenient expectations, like wanting access to your wealth or a say in how it's managed. These expectations might start small: asking for shared financial decisions or a budget to pursue personal passions. But left unchecked, they can spiral into full-blown "ideas" about fairness, independence, or, gasp, equity. A savvy billionaire knows that nipping these notions in the bud is crucial to maintaining control.

Step Two: Choose Carefully

The ideal spouse for a billionaire isn't just a compatible personality, they're an asset. This means selecting someone who aligns with your values (read: understands their place) and doesn't bring unnecessary complications to the table. While charm, beauty, and intelligence might be desirable traits, they pale in comparison to a potential partner's willingness to defer.

Look for signs of deference early on. Does this person accept the unspoken power dynamic, or do they bristle at the implications? Are they comfortable with the idea of you taking the lead in financial matters, or do they make noises about "collaboration"? A partner who challenges you in the honeymoon phase will likely become a full-blown liability down the line. Opt for someone who shows a natural inclination to appreciate, rather than question, your authority.

Of course, you'll want to vet their background thoroughly. Ideally, your partner should have enough privilege to feel secure but not so much that they bring their own "ideas" about entitlement to the table. The sweet spot is someone who's comfortable being adjacent to power without ever attempting to wield it. A solid trust fund baby with no ambition or a mild-mannered creative who just wants to "express themselves" without disrupting your empire are prime candidates.

Step Three: Control the Narrative

Once you've chosen your partner, it's crucial to establish the relationship narrative early. Set expectations about roles, responsibilities, and, most importantly, boundaries. Money conversations should happen before the wedding, ideally alongside a team of lawyers armed with ironclad pre-nuptial agreements. Present these agreements not as a lack of trust but as a "formality" necessary to protect what you've both worked so hard for (yes, you'll need to let them feel included in the "we" for now).

Position yourself as the benevolent provider, framing your control over the finances as a way to ensure stability and prosperity for both parties. Subtly suggest that financial independence isn't necessary because you're there to take care of everything. It's not manipulation, it's efficiency. Why would they want to get bogged down in the complexities of wealth management when they could focus on more fulfilling pursuits, like charity galas or redecorating the vacation home?

Communication here is key, but only the kind of communication that reinforces your position. The less said about shared decision-making, the better. Introduce the idea that you have their best interests at heart, while ensuring that their involvement in financial matters is minimal. The goal is to build a relationship dynamic where they feel grateful rather than entitled. Gratitude, after all, is the antidote to ambition.

Step Four: Subtly Manage Aspirations

A partner with too much ambition can spell trouble. While you might enjoy their drive initially, unchecked ambition can lead to independence, and independence can lead to demands. To avoid this, encourage their aspirations only insofar as they don't threaten your control. Hobbies? Absolutely. Philanthropy? Sure, as long as it's bankrolled by you. But career ambitions or entrepreneurial ventures? Proceed with caution. These pursuits might seem harmless at first, but they come with the risk of fostering a sense of autonomy.

The trick is to appear supportive while quietly steering them toward pursuits that reinforce their dependence on you. Suggest charitable endeavors that align with your brand or passion projects that require your funding and approval. Celebrate their interests as long as they remain secondary to your goals. If they do venture into a career, position yourself as their biggest cheerleader, but subtly remind them that their success wouldn't be possible without your resources and connections.

Step Five: Deploy Emotional Manipulation Sparingly

Even the most carefully chosen and managed spouse may, at some point, develop inconvenient ideas. When this happens, emotional manipulation can be an effective tool, but it must be wielded delicately. The goal is not to break their spirit but to gently redirect their thinking.

Use language that appeals to their sense of loyalty. Remind them of the sacrifices you've made to build your empire and how your decisions always have their best interests at heart. Frame any resistance as a misunderstanding rather than defiance. If they press for more control or question your judgment, suggest that their concerns stem from external pressures rather than genuine grievances. *"I know your friends mean well, but they don't understand what we're building together."* This positions you as the reasonable one, while subtly isolating them from influences that might stoke their ambitions.

If all else fails, a gesture of generosity can help reset the balance. A lavish gift, an extravagant trip, or a public display of affection can go a long way in reinforcing their gratitude and quelling dissent. After all, it's hard to complain when you're being whisked away to a private island, or so you hope.

Step Six: Accept the Emptiness

At this point, it's worth pausing to acknowledge the profound sadness of this entire endeavor. In your relentless quest to preserve wealth, you've reduced love to a series of calculations, prenuptial clauses, and manipulative tactics. You've traded vulnerability for control, intimacy for strategy, and connection for compliance. And while you tell yourself that you've won, that your empire remains secure and your partner remains loyal, you know deep down that you've lost something far more valuable.

The tragedy of this strategy is that it ensures no one will ever truly love you, at least not for who you are. They might love your wealth, your power, or even your carefully constructed persona, but they'll never love the person beneath the penthouse facade. And why should they? You've spent so much time building walls around your fortune that you've become unreachable, untouchable, unknowable.

But does it really matter? You're rich. Isn't that enough? In a world where wealth is the ultimate measure of success, the hollowness of your relationships is just a small price to pay. You can console yourself with yachts, private jets, and a portfolio of investments that will outlive you. Love may be fleeting, but compound interest is forever.

So go ahead, billionaire. Choose your spouse carefully. Manage their expectations, control the narrative, and preserve your empire at all costs. And when you find yourself alone in your mansion, wondering why no one truly understands you, remind yourself that this is what you wanted. After all, love is messy, unpredictable, and deeply human. Wealth, on the other hand, is safe, stable, and gloriously inhuman. Isn't that what you've been striving for all along?

Affairs of Convenience- Managing Relationships Without Messy Emotions

For a billionaire, relationships are rarely about love—they're about logistics. Real emotions are unpredictable, messy, and worst of all, uncontrollable. In your world, control isn't optional; it's the foundation of everything you do. So when it comes to personal relationships, the last thing you need is drama. Enter the *affair of convenience*: a calculated arrangement that offers companionship, intimacy, and perhaps even a touch of glamour, all without the tangled web of emotional baggage. It's not love, it's a transaction, one designed to be efficient, manageable, and above all, beneficial to your carefully curated life.

The first rule of an affair of convenience is clarity. Both parties must understand the terms of the arrangement. You're not here to build a life together; you're here to enjoy a mutually agreeable situation that aligns with your lifestyle. This means defining boundaries early: no expectations of exclusivity, no intrusive demands on your time, and certainly no emotional entanglements that might disrupt the carefully balanced ecosystem of your empire. While this might sound cold, it's actually quite practical. In a world where wealth and power are always under scrutiny, simplicity is your best friend.

Choosing the right partner is crucial. Ideally, this person should be attractive, charming, and socially adept enough to enhance your image but independent enough to avoid becoming a liability. They should have their own life, their own aspirations, ones that don't interfere with yours, and a shared understanding that their role is complementary, not central. The goal is to find someone who adds value without complication, someone who understands the arrangement for what it is and, more importantly, what it isn't.

Of course, even the most convenient relationships come with risks. Emotional boundaries can blur, especially when intimacy is involved. That's why regular communication is essential, not the kind that delves into feelings but the kind that reaffirms the practical nature of your connection. A casual, *"This is working well for us, isn't it?"* goes a long way in maintaining the status quo. Any sign of emotional attachment should be addressed swiftly and tactfully. The moment feelings start creeping in, the balance of power shifts, and for a billionaire, power is non-negotiable.

Discretion is another cornerstone of an affair of convenience. The last thing you need is a headline about your personal life overshadowing your professional accomplishments. NDAs are non-negotiable, signed and ironclad before the first martini is poured. Social media posts featuring you should be minimal, if allowed at all. The fewer people who know about your arrangement, the better. In public, keep things polished and polite; in private, keep things quiet and controlled. The goal is to avoid scandal while maintaining the illusion of a seamless personal life.

But let's not ignore the hollowness at the heart of it all. No matter how well you manage these arrangements, they lack the unpredictability, depth, and connection that define real relationships. You can tell yourself that you don't need messy emotions, that your life is better for the simplicity and order you've cultivated, but the truth is harder to swallow. Affairs of convenience are empty by design. They're placeholders for something deeper, something you've convinced yourself isn't worth the risk. The very walls you've built to protect yourself from emotional chaos have also insulated you from genuine intimacy.

Still, what does it matter? You're rich. In your world, companionship is just another asset, one you acquire and manage like anything else. And when this arrangement runs its course, you'll move on to the next, seamlessly replacing one convenient relationship with another. After all, the world is full of people willing to play their part for a taste of your lifestyle. There's no shortage of candidates for the role, and as long as you maintain control, the system works.

But late at night, when the house is quiet and the city below glimmers with lights, you might wonder what it's all for. You have everything you ever wanted, yet the emptiness persists, a quiet reminder that all the money in the world can't buy the one thing you've systematically avoided: vulnerability. And while you tell yourself that this is the price of success, a small, nagging voice might ask whether it was worth it. But you silence that voice, pour yourself another drink, and remind yourself that control is all that matters. Isn't it?

Legacy Relationships Partnering for Power, Not Passion

When you're a billionaire, love is optional, but legacy is mandatory. The choices you make about your partner aren't guided by passion, they're guided by strategy. A legacy relationship isn't about romance; it's about optics, influence, and ensuring that your empire remains intact and thriving. Passion is fleeting, but power? Power is forever. Partnering for power rather than passion means choosing someone who enhances your brand, expands your reach, and consolidates your control. It's not about building a life together; it's about building an empire that will endure long after you're gone.

The first step in crafting a legacy relationship is understanding its purpose. This isn't about finding "the one" or someone who "completes" you. You're not looking for soulmates or sparks, you're looking for synergy. Your partner is a reflection of you, a visible symbol of your values, ambitions, and priorities. Whether they come from a similarly wealthy family, wield political influence, or bring cultural cachet, their primary role is to elevate your status. In the game of legacy building, their contribution isn't emotional, it's tactical.

Your partner must fit seamlessly into the narrative you're constructing. If you're positioning yourself as a forward-thinking visionary, they should embody that same ethos. If your brand relies on old-world prestige, they should come with impeccable lineage or a touch of aristocratic charm. Legacy relationships are about compatibility, but not in the traditional sense. It's about ensuring their public image aligns perfectly with yours. Even their hobbies, style, and philanthropic interests should reflect and amplify your own. A mismatched partner isn't just a personal inconvenience, it's a liability to your legacy.

This level of calculation can feel transactional because it is. You're entering into a partnership, not a love story. That doesn't mean the relationship lacks mutual respect or affection; it simply means those elements are secondary to the bigger picture. You're both playing a role, one that benefits both parties in different ways. They gain access to your wealth, influence, and resources, and you gain their image, connections, and loyalty. It's a symbiotic arrangement, cold, perhaps, but undeniably effective.

Of course, this kind of relationship requires meticulous management. Like any other asset, it must be maintained, nurtured, and occasionally renegotiated. Your partner must understand the rules of engagement: no public disputes, no surprises, and no behavior that could undermine the empire. In return, they are handsomely rewarded with status, luxury, and the assurance that they are part of something larger than themselves. As long as they play their role, the arrangement thrives.

But let's not pretend there's anything remotely romantic about it. A legacy relationship is devoid of the unpredictability and intensity that defines real passion. There are no stolen glances, no midnight confessions, no heart-pounding moments of vulnerability. Instead, there are carefully planned photo ops, coordinated public appearances, and joint statements crafted by PR teams. It's a performance, one designed to convey unity and strength while concealing the hollow mechanics underneath. And while it might look perfect from the outside, you know better. The chemistry you project is a façade, as meticulously curated as the art collection hanging in your penthouse.

Yet, for all its cynicism, a legacy relationship does serve a purpose. It offers stability in a chaotic world, a constant in a life defined by ambition and relentless pursuit. And let's not ignore the practicality of it all. Passion can cloud judgment, but power sharpens focus. By partnering strategically, you avoid the pitfalls of emotional entanglement that could jeopardize your wealth or reputation. You don't fall victim to impulsive decisions because your relationship is built on logic, not feelings. It's a fortress, not a firework.

Still, there's an undeniable emptiness to it. In your pursuit of control and legacy, you've traded away something profound, the chance to truly connect with another person. You've built a life where every interaction is measured, every relationship a calculation. Even the person you share your bed with is part of the empire, not separate from it. You've achieved the ultimate power couple dynamic, but at what cost? When the cameras are off and the world stops watching, what's left between you? Do you even know the person standing beside you, or are they just another cog in the well-oiled machine of your legacy?

Chapter 10
Creating Legacy Without Effort

The Art of Vanity Projects- From Museums to Universities, How to Immortalize Yourself

For billionaires, wealth is not just a tool for living, it's a tool for transcending mortality. While mere mortals measure their legacies in memories and gravestones, billionaires have the resources to ensure their names are etched into the cultural, academic, and physical landscapes of society. Vanity projects, museums, university buildings, research centers, hospitals, are the ultimate status symbols, combining philanthropy with an unspoken promise of eternal fame. These are not simple acts of generosity; they are monuments to ego, strategically designed to say, *"I mattered. I was here."* The art of the vanity project lies not in giving back but in ensuring that what you give comes back to you tenfold, in recognition, reverence, and immortality.

Step One: Choose Your Arena

The first step in crafting a vanity project is selecting the right domain for your name to shine. Museums are a classic choice, offering the perfect blend of prestige and public visibility. Whether it's funding a wing in an existing institution or building an entirely new museum from scratch, the goal is to align your name with culture and sophistication. Nothing says *"I'm a patron of the arts"* quite like slapping your last name on a building that houses priceless artifacts you'll never fully understand.

If art isn't your speed, consider universities. An endowed chair, a library, or an entire school of thought can bear your name for centuries, ensuring that every aspiring scholar whispers your name while complaining about tuition fees. A billionaire-funded university wing isn't just a donation, it's a power move. It positions you as a tastemaker in education and subtly implies that your wisdom and values are as timeless as the pursuit of knowledge itself.

Hospitals and research centers offer a slightly different flavor of immortality, one that pairs well with the rhetoric of "giving back." By funding medical advancements or cutting-edge research, you position yourself as a savior of humanity. Of course, whether those advancements actually serve the public or quietly protect your investments is beside the point. The building exists, your name is on it, and the photo ops are glorious.

Step Two: Build the Narrative

A vanity project is only as good as the story it tells. You're not just funding a wing or erecting a building; you're creating a narrative of vision, altruism, and impact. This requires careful curation of your motivations. Publicly, you should emphasize your commitment to the greater good, your love for art, your passion for education, or your dedication to curing diseases. Privately, of course, the goal is to secure your legacy.

The narrative should highlight your journey: how you started from humble beginnings (even if you didn't), how your success allows you to give back (even if you're only giving a fraction of your wealth), and how this project reflects your personal values (even if those values are entirely fabricated for PR purposes). The key is to make it seem like the project was inevitable, a natural extension of your life's work rather than a carefully calculated branding exercise.

Don't underestimate the importance of naming. A project named after you is the ultimate flex, but if subtlety is required, consider naming it after a family member or a vague ideal. *The [Your Last Name] Institute for Excellence* or *The Legacy Foundation* strikes the right balance of grandeur and humility.

Step Three: Involve the Right People

No vanity project succeeds without the right partnerships. This is where universities, museums, and nonprofits come into play. These institutions are often eager, desperate, even, for funding, and they're more than happy to bend to your will in exchange for your financial largesse. Leverage this desperation to ensure that your project aligns perfectly with your vision, which, let's be honest, is mostly about making your name synonymous with greatness. Want a say in the design of the building, the programming of the institution, or the hiring of key personnel? Of course you do—and with enough zeros in your check, you'll get it.
Ensure the institutions you partner with understand the magnitude of

your generosity. You're not just funding a wing or a center; you're shaping the future (or so they'll say at the ribbon-cutting ceremony). Surround yourself with architects, curators, and directors who know how to turn your money into something that screams *legacy*. Be the visionary in the room, nodding thoughtfully as experts pitch ideas, and then make it abundantly clear that your final approval hinges on whether they're sufficiently honoring *you*. After all, it's not really a vanity project unless it revolves around, well, *your vanity*.

Step Four: The Grand Opening

The culmination of any vanity project is the unveiling, and this moment must be nothing short of spectacular. The grand opening is your chance to showcase your "philanthropy" while basking in the adoration of the public, your peers, and the institution you just funded. A lavish ceremony is essential, think champagne, speeches, and a press release that ensures your generosity trends for days. Bonus points if you can secure a celebrity or politician to speak on your behalf, cementing your importance not only to the project but to society as a whole.

Your speech should be a masterclass in performative humility. Open with a nod to the institution and its leaders, then segue into how this project reflects your lifelong values. Drop a line about how humbled you are to be in a position to give back, even as the building's massive facade looms behind you, emblazoned with your name. Close with an optimistic statement about the future, ensuring that everyone present leaves feeling like they just witnessed history, or, at the very least, your carefully choreographed version of it.

Step Five: Secure the Legacy

Once the project is live, the real work begins. Your vanity project isn't just a one-time gesture; it's a long-term investment in your immortality. Ensure the institution maintains the standards you set, even if that means hovering over their decisions for years to come. Remember, your name is now attached to this entity, so its success, or failure, reflects on you. Establish an endowment or foundation to keep the project well-funded and ensure that your influence persists long after you've exited the stage (or the planet).
Meanwhile, use the project to bolster your image. Whenever your name appears in the news for less-than-flattering reasons, say, a labor

scandal or tax evasion allegations, point to your institution as evidence of your good character. *"How could someone who built the [Your Last Name] Center for Human Progress possibly be greedy?"* The project becomes both a shield and a sword, deflecting criticism while reinforcing your reputation as a benevolent titan.

The Vanity Trap

Despite the grandeur, there's an inescapable emptiness to all of this. Beneath the plaques and press releases lies a grim reality: your legacy project isn't about leaving a mark on the world, it's about leaving a mark on yourself. These museums, universities, and research centers aren't monuments to progress or enlightenment; they're monuments to your ego. Sure, people will walk through the halls of your institute or read books from your endowed library, but their admiration isn't for the institution, it's for the name slapped across its front. The hollowness grows deeper when you realize that, for all your money and influence, this is the best you could do to fight mortality. Perhaps in a hundred years, people will still visit your museum or study at your university. But will they care about *you*, or will your name become just another decorative inscription, as meaningful as the worn marble plaques commemorating philanthropists of centuries past?

A Monument to the Times

In the end, the art of vanity projects isn't about making the world better, it's about making sure the world remembers you. It's an act of desperation masquerading as altruism, a multi-million-dollar cry for relevance in a world that will inevitably move on. But in the age of obscene wealth and shallow values, what better way to immortalize yourself than by building a temple to your ego and calling it progress? So, go ahead. Fund the museum, endow the university, cure a disease, or at least pretend to. Your legacy won't be a testament to your character but to the sheer audacity of a life lived in pursuit of power, fame, and control. And when future generations look up at the towering edifice of your vanity project, they'll see exactly what you wanted them to see: your name, your wealth, your mark on the world. Whether they admire it or laugh at it, well, that's up to them.

Philanthropic Legacy: Ensuring Your Name Lives Forever

Philanthropy is often touted as the noblest expression of wealth, but for billionaires, it's rarely as altruistic as it appears. Sure, writing massive checks to fund universities, hospitals, and research initiatives looks great on paper, but the true motivation often has less to do with helping humanity and more to do with ensuring that your name echoes through the ages. A philanthropic legacy is not just an act of generosity; it's a carefully calculated investment in immortality. Done correctly, it guarantees that long after your yacht has rusted and your offshore accounts have been forgotten, your name will live on in lecture halls, museum plaques, and hospital wings.

The art of building a philanthropic legacy begins with one simple realization: it's not about solving problems, it's about branding. You're not funding initiatives to cure diseases or educate future generations because it's the right thing to do. You're doing it because it ensures your wealth is synonymous with progress, innovation, and benevolence. The key is to frame your giving as transformative while keeping one eye firmly on how it benefits you. After all, philanthropy without recognition is just a loss on the balance sheet.

Step One: The Right Cause

Choosing the right cause is critical to building your legacy. The ideal philanthropic endeavor is one that aligns with your public image while offering maximum visibility. If you're a tech billionaire, funding STEM education or artificial intelligence research is a natural fit, signaling that your generosity is as cutting-edge as your empire. If your wealth stems from real estate or finance, affordable housing or economic development initiatives tie neatly into your narrative as a builder of communities or an architect of prosperity.

Avoid controversial or overly niche causes that could detract from your reputation. You're not here to challenge norms or spark difficult conversations, you're here to look good. Focus on projects that offer universal appeal: curing cancer, combating climate change (with minimal personal sacrifice), or fostering innovation in areas where the results can be easily quantified and celebrated. A billion-dollar donation to eradicate malaria sounds much more impressive than quietly funding local food banks, even if the latter might actually help more people.

Step Two: Naming Rights

When it comes to philanthropy, the golden rule is simple: no name, no deal. You're not giving away millions, or billions, without ensuring that your contribution is permanently enshrined in stone, steel, or academic curricula. Insist on naming rights for every project you fund, whether it's a university building, a hospital wing, or a fellowship program. A donation without a name is a wasted opportunity to cement your place in history.

Naming conventions should strike a balance between grandeur and humility. *The [Your Name] Center for Excellence* or *The [Your Family Name] Institute for Innovation* exudes prestige without seeming too self-congratulatory. Avoid overtly egotistical titles unless you're fully embracing your inner narcissist, *"The Monument to My Greatness"* probably won't resonate well with your PR team, though it might be closer to the truth.

Step Three: The PR Machine

No philanthropic legacy is complete without a robust public relations campaign. The narrative must frame you as a visionary leader who, despite immense wealth, has never lost sight of the common good. Carefully curated press releases, interviews, and public appearances should emphasize your passion for the cause and your commitment to making a difference. Never miss an opportunity to appear at the ribbon-cutting ceremony or groundbreaking event, preferably with a teary-eyed speech about how much this means to you.

The real genius of philanthropy lies in its ability to reframe criticism. If anyone dares to point out how your fortune was built, whether through environmental degradation, exploitative labor practices, or tax avoidance, you can redirect the conversation. *"Yes, but look at the cancer research I've funded." "Sure, but think of the scholarships my foundation has provided."* Your philanthropy doesn't erase the harm you've caused, but it gives the public a shiny distraction, a narrative of redemption that keeps you above reproach.

Step Four: Endowments and Foundations

True immortality requires infrastructure. A one-time donation might get your name in the papers, but an endowment or foundation ensures that your influence, and your name, will persist for generations. Endowments provide ongoing funding to universities, museums, or hospitals in your name, while foundations allow you to exert control over how your wealth is used long after you're gone. These institutions are not just vehicles for philanthropy; they're monuments to your values (or at least the values you want people to think you hold).

Foundations, in particular, offer a unique blend of power and immortality. By setting up your own, you retain significant control over where the money goes, shaping the future in your image. They also provide a convenient tax shelter, allowing you to avoid contributing to public funds while appearing altruistic. It's a win-win: you get the glory of giving without actually giving it to, you know, *the government*.

Step Five: The Performance of Humility

To solidify your legacy, you must perfect the delicate art of performative humility. When speaking about your contributions, use language that downplays your role while elevating the cause. Statements like, *"I'm just honored to support the brilliant minds doing this work,"* or, *"This isn't about me, it's about what we can achieve together,"* are staples of the billionaire philanthropist's repertoire. Of course, it *is* about you, but no one needs to know that.

Humility should also extend to your lifestyle, or at least appear to. Consider the occasional public nod to modesty, like wearing understated clothing at charity events or claiming to live simply despite owning three yachts. These gestures reinforce the narrative that your wealth hasn't changed you, even as you build entire wings of universities dedicated to your name.

Step Six: The Hollow Truth

For all its grandeur, the pursuit of a philanthropic legacy carries an undeniable emptiness. Deep down, you know the truth: your giving is as much about ego as it is about impact. Your name on a hospital wing or a university building doesn't solve the problems that your wealth and power helped create. It's a bandage, not a cure, a way to paper over the cracks in your public image while ensuring that your legacy isn't one of greed alone.

The irony, of course, is that your name will endure, but likely not in the way you intended. As time passes, the world will forget the specifics of your philanthropy, reducing you to a plaque on a wall or a footnote in a textbook. The institutions you funded may persist, but their connection to you will fade, swallowed by the endless march of time. Your legacy, carefully crafted and obsessively managed, will become little more than a curiosity, a remnant of a life spent chasing immortality.

The Billionaire's Dilemma

In the end, a philanthropic legacy is less about ensuring your name lives forever and more about delaying the inevitable realization that no one truly lasts. You can fund libraries, cure diseases, and build monuments, but you can't escape the fundamental truth: wealth doesn't make you eternal, it just buys you a slightly longer spotlight. And while the world may marvel at your generosity today, it will eventually move on, as it always does.

So, billionaire, write the checks, cut the ribbons, and bask in the applause. Build your legacy, brick by brick, knowing full well that it's a castle of sand. Because in the grand scheme of things, your name, no matter how many times it's engraved in marble, will someday be just another whisper in the wind.

Memoirs No One Asked For- Writing the Narrative Before History Does

Writing your memoir as a billionaire isn't about documenting the truth, it's about controlling the narrative before anyone else does. History is subjective, and when your fortune and influence inevitably attract scrutiny, the last thing you want is for someone else to tell your story. A memoir, then, isn't just a book—it's a weapon, a preemptive strike against criticism, and a gilded monument to your carefully crafted persona. After all, why let facts get in the way of a good legacy?

The first rule of billionaire memoirs is simple: frame your life as a masterpiece of perseverance and genius. It doesn't matter if your empire was built on inherited wealth, market manipulation, or exploitation. What matters is how you tell it. Your story should open with vivid imagery of your "humble beginnings," no matter how far from humble they actually were. Did you grow up in a mansion? Reframe it as a "modest home filled with love and dreams." Did you attend elite private schools? Focus instead on how much pressure you felt to succeed. The goal is relatability, even if your life was as relatable as a golden unicorn.

Next, position yourself as the protagonist in a heroic narrative. Every challenge you faced should be exaggerated into an insurmountable obstacle that only your unparalleled determination could overcome. Maybe your first business failed, but conveniently omit the family loan that allowed you to start over. Highlight long hours and sleepless nights, even if you had a team of assistants working around the clock. Your readers don't need the truth, they need a story that inspires, one that glosses over systemic advantages and portrays you as a self-made pioneer.

Of course, no billionaire memoir is complete without a chapter, or twenty, on your "philanthropy." This section should be an ode to your generosity, focusing on the causes you've supported and the lives you've changed. Never mind that your donations are often tax-deductible or strategically designed to improve your public image. Present yourself as a visionary giver, someone who has used their fortune to change the world. Sprinkle in anecdotes about heartfelt encounters with the people you've helped, even if those moments were entirely orchestrated by your PR team.

The tone of your memoir should also strike a balance between modesty and grandeur. You're not just writing about your life; you're defining your legacy. Use language that frames your achievements as transformative while downplaying the collateral damage. If critics have accused you of monopolistic practices or labor abuses, dismiss those concerns as "misunderstandings" or "the cost of innovation." Be sure to emphasize how deeply you value your employees—perhaps dedicate a paragraph or two to the Christmas bonuses you once handed out. The point isn't accuracy; it's control.

To truly immortalize yourself, devote a significant portion of the book to "lessons learned." Share your wisdom with the world, even if it's as shallow as *"Follow your dreams"* or *"Never give up."* Pepper these chapters with quotes that sound profound but mean little, ensuring they're Instagram-ready for maximum cultural saturation. Position yourself as not only a business titan but a philosopher-king, someone whose insights will guide generations to come.

The memoir should conclude with a triumphant reflection on your legacy. Talk about your "lasting impact" on society, your "commitment to the greater good," and your hope that future generations will carry on your vision. Avoid any mention of controversies, failures, or the systems that allowed you to hoard wealth while others suffered. Instead, leave readers with a sense of awe, ensuring that your name is forever associated with greatness, not greed.

And yet, for all its grandeur, the billionaire memoir is ultimately a hollow endeavor. You're not writing it to connect with readers or share meaningful truths; you're writing it to shield yourself from history's judgment. It's not an act of vulnerability, it's an act of vanity, a desperate attempt to rewrite the story before anyone else can tell it. Deep down, you know that this book won't change the world, but it might, just might, convince a few people that you deserved your fortune.

So, go ahead. Write your memoir. Fill it with tales of triumph, generosity, and wisdom. And when the critics call it a self-serving fantasy, remember: history is written by the rich, and as long as you're the one holding the pen, the narrative will always be yours. Even if no one asked for it.

Family Wealth Planning- Keeping Your Empire Intact Across Generations

Building an empire is one thing, but keeping it intact across generations? That's the real legacy. Without careful planning, your fortune could fall victim to taxes, mismanagement, or, worst of all, the whims of heirs who lack your vision (or your discipline). Family wealth planning isn't just a matter of spreadsheets and trusts, it's about preserving control, maintaining influence, and ensuring that your empire doesn't crumble the moment you're no longer around to manage it.

The cornerstone of generational wealth planning is creating structures that protect your assets while minimizing risk. Trusts are essential, offering a way to pass down wealth without handing over full control. You can set up conditions, like requiring heirs to meet certain educational benchmarks or prove their competence in managing funds, ensuring that your money doesn't fall into the hands of someone who thinks "investment" means buying NFTs. Family offices are another key tool, consolidating financial management into a centralized operation to safeguard your empire's stability.

But wealth isn't just about money, it's about values. A legacy can't survive if future generations don't share your vision for stewardship. Family meetings, educational programs, and even retreats can instill the principles that built your fortune, from entrepreneurship to philanthropy. These events aren't just bonding opportunities, they're training sessions for the future CEOs, board members, and decision-makers who will carry your empire forward.

Finally, plan for your absence. Succession planning ensures that the transition of power is smooth, even if your heirs are less capable or interested in leadership. Appoint trusted advisors to oversee the process, minimizing the risk of internal squabbles or disastrous decision-making.

Because in the end, family wealth planning isn't just about keeping your fortune intact, it's about ensuring that your empire reflects your vision, long after you're gone. After all, if your legacy can't survive a single generation, did it ever truly matter?

Chapter 11
Embracing Your Inner Supervillain

Why Being the Villain Pays- Leaning Into Public Fear

Not every billionaire gets to play the hero, nor should they want to. In a world increasingly skeptical of wealth and power, being feared can often be more effective, and more profitable, than being loved. Villainy, when embraced strategically, isn't just about reveling in the public's disdain; it's about wielding fear as a tool to protect your empire, influence public perception, and, yes, maximize profits. The trick isn't to fight the villain narrative, it's to own it, weaponize it, and turn it into your greatest asset. After all, every empire needs its Darth Vader.

The first rule of leaning into public fear is understanding that it's not personal, it's business. The public's mistrust of billionaires is rooted in a cocktail of envy, suspicion, and genuine concern over inequality, but none of that changes the game you're playing. Fear isn't an obstacle to overcome; it's leverage. When people are afraid of you, whether it's because of your market dominance, your political influence, or your sheer disregard for criticism, they're less likely to challenge you directly. Fear creates distance, and distance creates power. By leaning into your villainous reputation, you make it clear that you're untouchable, a force too large to topple and too cunning to outmaneuver.

Villains, by definition, control the narrative, and that's where the payoff begins. If the world sees you as ruthless, why not use that to your advantage? Ruthlessness can be reframed as decisiveness, a willingness to make the tough calls that others can't stomach. Layoffs? Market monopolies? Crushing smaller competitors? These aren't acts of greed; they're bold moves that ensure the survival of your company—and by extension, the economy (or so you'll claim). When people fear your power, they're less likely to scrutinize the mechanics of how you wield it. Your audacity becomes part of the legend, reinforcing the idea that you're an unstoppable force in a world of mediocrity.

Of course, being the villain doesn't mean being sloppy. Public fear can backfire if it tips into outright hatred. The key is to cultivate a reputation as the necessary evil, someone whose actions, while controversial, are ultimately justified by the results. This requires careful PR management. Frame your decisions as sacrifices for the greater good, positioning yourself as the lone wolf willing to make unpopular choices for the survival of your industry, or humanity itself. Whether or not it's true is irrelevant; what matters is that the narrative sticks.

Take a page from history: villains often outlast their critics. The robber barons of the Gilded Age were vilified for their ruthless exploitation, but today, names like Carnegie and Rockefeller are synonymous with philanthropy and progress. How did they achieve this transformation? By doubling down on their power in the short term and strategically softening their image in the long term. You, too, can play both sides of the villain coin. While the world reels from your market dominance or political lobbying, quietly fund a hospital wing or an educational initiative. These gestures don't erase your actions, but they create a counter-narrative, muddying the waters enough to keep your legacy intact.

Villainy also pays in the boardroom. A fearsome reputation can cow competitors and embolden allies. If rival companies know you'll crush them without hesitation, they're less likely to challenge you directly. And if your employees understand that loyalty is non-negotiable, they'll work harder to stay in your good graces. Fear isn't just a tool for managing the public, it's a weapon for maintaining internal control. People might not love you, but they'll respect your power, and in business, respect often matters more than affection.

Public fear also allows you to control the pace of change. When people view you as a necessary evil, they're less likely to demand radical reforms. You become the devil they know, a stabilizing force in a chaotic world. Politicians hesitate to target you too aggressively, fearing the economic fallout of your potential retaliation. Activists, meanwhile, focus on easier targets, leaving your empire relatively unscathed. Fear creates inertia, and inertia is the billionaire's best friend.

But let's not ignore the personal perks of embracing the villain role. There's a certain freedom in owning your reputation. Heroes are held to impossibly high standards, their every misstep magnified. Villains, on the other hand, are expected to behave badly. This gives you room to maneuver, to act boldly without the constraints of moral expectation. You're not trying to be liked, which means you're free to do what needs to be done, no matter how unpopular it may be.

And while some might argue that this strategy is cynical, the truth is that fear and admiration often go hand in hand. People may resent your wealth and power, but they also can't look away. They watch your every move, fascinated by your audacity and the sheer scale of your ambition. Villains don't just inspire fear, they inspire awe. You become a larger-than-life figure, someone who transcends the petty squabbles of everyday existence. In a world obsessed with personalities, being a villain is often more memorable than being a hero.

Of course, this path isn't without its risks. Lean too far into villainy, and you risk alienating everyone, employees, allies, even your loyal consumers. The key is to maintain a delicate balance between fear and fascination, ensuring that your power is respected but not universally despised. This requires constant recalibration, a careful dance of PR campaigns, public gestures of goodwill, and moments of strategic humility. The goal is to remain untouchable without becoming irredeemable.

Ultimately, being the villain isn't just a role, it's a strategy. It's about recognizing that fear is as powerful a currency as wealth, and wielding it with precision. It's about understanding that public outrage, while uncomfortable, can be turned into leverage. And it's about embracing the reality that in a world where power is everything, being feared often pays far better than being loved. So lean in. Own it. And let the world marvel at the empire you've built, even if they're too afraid to admit it.

Owning the Narrative- Spinning Your Ruthlessness as Necessary for Progress

In a world that increasingly scrutinizes wealth and power, ruthlessness is not just a survival skill, it's a cornerstone of success. But being ruthless alone isn't enough; you have to convince the world that your calculated, sometimes brutal decisions are not acts of greed or malice, but necessary steps toward progress. Owning the narrative means taking control of how your actions are perceived, shaping the story so that your ambition, domination, and relentlessness appear not only justified but essential for the greater good.

This isn't about telling the truth, it's about telling *your* truth, the version of events that reframes ruthless decisions as bold leadership. It's about creating a narrative so compelling that people stop asking whether your methods were ethical and start marveling at how your actions propelled humanity forward. After all, progress doesn't come from playing nice, it comes from breaking the rules, disrupting the status quo, and doing what others won't. Or so your story will go.

Step 1: Rebrand Ruthlessness as Visionary Boldness

The first step in spinning your ruthlessness is to reframe it as the mark of a visionary. To the world, you're not crushing competitors or laying off thousands of workers, you're making tough decisions for the sake of innovation and efficiency. Use language that elevates your actions to a higher plane. You didn't monopolize an industry; you streamlined it. You didn't push smaller players out; you created a more robust and sustainable market. Words like *"optimization," "disruption,"* and *"restructuring"* are your best friends, masking the harshness of your decisions with a veneer of corporate sophistication.

The key is to portray yourself as someone willing to make sacrifices for the greater good. Frame your actions as necessary steps toward progress that others were too timid to take. If anyone dares to criticize you, point out that real change requires courage and that courage often looks like ruthlessness from the outside. *"I don't make decisions to be liked, I make them to drive results,"* you'll say, turning critiques of your methods into applause for your conviction.

Step 2: Emphasize the Ends Over the Means

People are far more forgiving of questionable methods if the results are impressive enough. Shift the focus away from how you achieved success and onto what you achieved. Did you lay off 20,000 workers to save your company? Highlight how that decision ensured the survival of the business, protected investors, and paved the way for future job creation. Did your company bulldoze local businesses? Emphasize how your streamlined operations brought lower prices to millions of consumers. The narrative should always center on the benefits your ruthlessness created, not the collateral damage it left behind.

This approach works especially well when paired with a long-term vision. The bigger the dream, the more willing people are to forgive the shortcuts you took to achieve it. You're not just cutting corners, you're building the future. Turn every criticism into proof that you're thinking beyond the here and now, reminding people that history will vindicate you, even if the present moment feels uncomfortable.

Step 3: Align Yourself with Progress

To truly own the narrative, position yourself as an agent of progress. This means associating your brand with causes that carry broad public appeal: innovation, sustainability, equality, or any issue that makes you look like a forward-thinking leader. By aligning your ruthless actions with these ideals, you shift the conversation from "What did they do?" to "What are they working toward?"

For instance, if your company is accused of exploiting workers, emphasize how your actions are driving advancements in automation, which will ultimately improve productivity and quality of life for everyone. If your environmental practices are criticized, point to your investments in green technology and frame them as part of a broader commitment to sustainability. The key is to create a narrative where your ruthlessness isn't just justified, it's essential for solving the world's biggest problems.

Step 4: Master the Art of Preemptive Framing

The best way to own the narrative is to get ahead of it. Don't wait for the media or your critics to define your actions, frame them yourself.

When announcing controversial decisions, provide a ready-made story that emphasizes your intentions and downplays the consequences. Pair layoffs with a pledge to reinvest in the community. Pair monopolistic behavior with a promise to use your market position to lower costs for consumers. Make it clear that every tough call is part of a larger plan that benefits society in ways only you can see.

Preemptive framing also involves owning your flaws before others can weaponize them. Acknowledge your reputation for ruthlessness, but spin it as a strength. *"I know some people see my decisions as harsh, but I see them as necessary,"* you might say. This not only deflates criticism but also reinforces your image as a fearless leader who prioritizes results over popularity.

Step 5: Use Philanthropy as a Counterbalance

Philanthropy is one of the most effective tools for spinning ruthlessness into progress. By funding hospitals, universities, or environmental initiatives, you create a narrative that counters accusations of greed or exploitation. Your philanthropic efforts don't need to outweigh the harm caused by your actions, they just need to distract from it. When critics call you ruthless, point to your donations as proof of your commitment to making the world a better place.

Philanthropy also provides an opportunity to double down on your narrative. If your ruthlessness in business leads to criticism, use your charitable work to argue that your wealth is being used for good. *"Yes, I've made tough decisions, but they've allowed me to fund cancer research, educational programs, and clean energy solutions,"* you'll say. In doing so, you position yourself not just as a billionaire but as a force for progress.

Step 6: Create a Mythology

Ruthlessness becomes palatable when it's wrapped in mythology. Craft a story about yourself that portrays your actions as the result of extraordinary vision, resilience, and sacrifice. Highlight the challenges you overcame, the risks you took, and the sleepless nights you endured to achieve your success. The more you humanize yourself, the harder it becomes for critics to reduce you to a caricature of greed.

This mythology should also include a clear sense of purpose. You're not ruthless for the sake of it, you're ruthless because you have a responsibility to lead. Position yourself as a trailblazer, someone who isn't afraid to break the rules to build a better future. Even if people disagree with your methods, they'll respect your conviction.

Step 7: Own the Criticism

No narrative is complete without acknowledging its dissenters. Embrace the criticism, but reframe it as proof of your impact. *"If people aren't questioning you, you're not pushing hard enough,"* you might say, turning skepticism into a badge of honor. The most successful narratives don't ignore controversy, they incorporate it, using it as evidence that the stakes are high and the challenges are worth tackling.

By owning the criticism, you also neutralize it. When someone accuses you of being ruthless, you can respond, *"I understand why people feel that way, but I'm focused on the bigger picture."* This approach deflects negativity while reinforcing your image as a leader who's willing to weather the storm for the sake of progress.

The Villain as Visionary

Ultimately, owning the narrative isn't about convincing everyone that you're a hero—it's about redefining what it means to be a leader. Ruthlessness, when framed correctly, becomes a virtue: a sign of strength, clarity, and commitment to results. By controlling the narrative, you ensure that your legacy isn't tarnished by controversy but elevated by the perception of bold leadership.

So lean into it. Be ruthless, but be strategic. And when history looks back on your actions, make sure it sees not a tyrant, but a visionary who did what needed to be done to move the world forward, on your terms.

Symbols of Power- Designing Your Empire to Intimidate

In the world of billionaires, wealth is more than a resource, it's a weapon. To maintain your dominance, you don't just need an empire; you need an empire that *looks* like an empire. The symbols of power you create, buildings, logos, headquarters, and even personal style, aren't just aesthetic choices. They're statements of authority designed to remind the world of your influence. These symbols intimidate competitors, inspire loyalty in subordinates, and subtly remind everyone else that you operate on a plane they can never hope to reach.

Building Your Fortress

The physical manifestations of your power start with your headquarters. This isn't just an office, it's a throne, a declaration of your position at the top of the food chain. The architecture should embody dominance: towering skyscrapers, sleek modernist designs, or fortress-like structures that exude unapproachability. Glass walls say transparency (even when there's none); stark lines and imposing entrances convey authority. Ideally, your headquarters should dwarf the surrounding buildings, making it clear that your empire literally overshadows everything else.

Location matters, too. Position your headquarters in the heart of a bustling financial district or atop a hill overlooking a city. You're not just running a business, you're ruling a kingdom. If you're truly bold, your headquarters should be visible from miles away, a looming presence that reminds everyone who's really in charge.

Inside, the design should balance opulence and intimidation. Polished marble floors, enormous boardrooms, and dramatic lighting make your workspace feel like a temple to power. Art collections, rare artifacts, and imposing sculptures can reinforce your brand as a patron of culture, or simply as someone too wealthy to care about price tags. Even the layout of your office should signal your status: long, intimidating walkways to your desk, soaring ceilings, and furniture that dwarfs visitors.

Logos and Branding

Your company's logo isn't just a design, it's a sigil, a symbol that people immediately associate with wealth, power, and influence. Think Apple's minimalist bite, Amazon's smirking arrow, or Tesla's futuristic simplicity. These are more than logos; they're statements of dominance in their industries. Your logo should strike a similar chord, combining simplicity with boldness. Whether it's a monogram, a geometric design, or an abstract shape, it should be instantly recognizable and imbued with gravitas.

Colors matter too. Black, gold, and silver are perennial favorites in the language of power, elegant, timeless, and unmistakably high-status. Avoid colors that suggest vulnerability or playfulness; your brand should command respect, not invite whimsy. Fonts should follow suit, favoring clean, bold lines that project stability and strength. The goal is to ensure that every time someone sees your logo, they feel a little smaller, a little more aware of your towering presence.

Corporate Aesthetics

Beyond the logo, the overall branding of your empire should be cohesive and intimidating. Your website, marketing materials, and even your social media accounts should reflect a singular aesthetic of dominance. No typos, no low-budget photography, and definitely no attempts to seem *too* relatable. Your online presence should exude polish and precision, reinforcing the idea that you're running a well-oiled machine.

Even your employees can serve as symbols of your power. Dress codes should reflect the seriousness of your empire, favoring tailored suits, minimalist uniforms, or other high-status attire. When your workforce looks like they stepped out of a corporate utopia, it sends a message to the world: this isn't just a business, it's an institution.

Yachts, Jets, and Residences

Symbols of power aren't limited to the workplace. Your personal possessions, yachts, private jets, and sprawling estates, are equally important in projecting your dominance. A yacht isn't just a luxury; it's a floating palace that doubles as a status symbol. It should be large enough to host dignitaries, celebrities, and, of course, the occasional

Instagram-worthy charity gala.

Private jets serve a similar purpose. The more customized and exclusive, the better. Think interiors decked out with custom leather seating, rare wood finishes, and enough advanced technology to make passengers feel like they're stepping into the future. Bonus points if your jet's tail features a custom design tied to your empire's branding.

Residences, too, should reflect your status. Multiple properties across global hotspots are a given, but each one should be unique. A Manhattan penthouse with panoramic city views, a Mediterranean villa perched atop cliffs, and a mountain retreat that looks like a Bond villain's lair—they're not just homes; they're territorial markers that reinforce your global reach.

Personal Style as Intimidation

Your appearance is a living symbol of your power. The way you dress, speak, and carry yourself can intimidate rivals and inspire loyalty. Every detail matters. Suits should be tailored to perfection, subtly hinting at exclusivity without shouting it. Watches, jewelry, and accessories should be understated but clearly expensive—Patek Philippe over Rolex, for example.

Even your language should project control. Speak with confidence, keep your tone measured, and master the art of saying little while implying much. In interviews or public appearances, focus on creating an aura of unshakeable authority. The goal is to make every interaction feel like a privilege for the other party, reminding them that they're in the presence of someone extraordinary.

The Fear Factor

At the heart of all these symbols is the emotion they evoke: awe, envy, and most importantly, fear. The intimidation factor isn't just about aesthetics; it's about ensuring that everyone who encounters your empire, whether it's a competitor, a partner, or a critic, feels a sense of your overwhelming presence.

Fear creates space, and space creates power. Competitors hesitate to challenge you, partners tread carefully to stay in your good graces, and critics find themselves overwhelmed by the sheer scale of your dominance. Your symbols of power aren't just for show, they're your first line of defense, discouraging anyone from even thinking about taking you on.

Longevity Through Design

Symbols of power also serve a long-term purpose: ensuring your legacy. A headquarters can become a landmark, a logo can become iconic, and a well-crafted image can persist long after you're gone. The more enduring your symbols, the harder it becomes for history to forget you.

In the end, designing your empire isn't just about running a business, it's about creating a legacy of control, authority, and influence. Symbols of power remind the world that you're not just playing the game, you've already won. And as long as they stand, so does your dominance.

If They Hate You, You're Doing It Right- The Metrics of Unapologetic Success

In the world of billionaires, universal approval isn't just unnecessary, it's impossible. The higher you climb, the louder the critics become. But here's the secret: their hate isn't a problem; it's a metric. If they hate you, it's because you're succeeding on a scale they can't ignore. Embracing this truth is the key to unapologetic success. Approval is for the small-minded; impact, even when it provokes resentment, is for the bold.

Hate as a Measure of Impact

First, let's get one thing straight: no one criticizes irrelevance. The very fact that people hate you means you've captured their attention. When your decisions affect industries, economies, or even global policies, someone will always have a problem with it. Layoffs? Market domination? Buying a social media platform and turning it into your personal soapbox? These moves spark outrage precisely because they're consequential. The more people hate you, the more undeniable your presence becomes. Hate isn't the antithesis of success, it's the evidence of it. Use this to your advantage. Measure the intensity of criticism not as a sign that you've overstepped, but as proof that you've disrupted the status quo. If your competitors are seething and social media is aflame with outrage, congratulations, you've left your mark. Critics mean you've moved the needle, and movement is the essence of success.

Turning Outrage into Obsession

Here's the ironic thing about being hated: it often breeds obsession. People may despise your methods, but they can't stop watching. They dissect your every move, amplify your influence through their outrage, and keep your name in the headlines. The key is to harness this energy, turning their attention into fuel for your brand. When they criticize your luxury lifestyle, post a photo of your new yacht. When they accuse you of wielding too much influence, remind them of the global reach of your empire. Every act of defiance reinforces the idea that you're operating on a level they can only dream of. Hate isn't just a reaction, it's free publicity. Lean into it.

The Strength of Polarization

Polarization isn't a weakness; it's a strength. Trying to please everyone dilutes your message and weakens your brand. By embracing polarization, you create a base of loyal supporters who admire your audacity just as much as others loathe it. Your detractors will call you arrogant, selfish, or even dangerous, but your supporters will see you as bold, decisive, and visionary. This dynamic is particularly valuable in business. While critics scream into the void, your supporters buy your products, invest in your ventures, and defend you against backlash. By owning your identity and refusing to apologize for your success, you solidify your power base. Hate isn't a liability, it's a dividing line that separates those who matter from those who don't.

Letting Go of Approval

Perhaps the hardest lesson of unapologetic success is learning to let go of approval. The desire to be liked is human, but billionaires don't have the luxury of being merely human. Approval is a trap, one that tempts you to compromise your vision to satisfy others. True success requires the courage to ignore this impulse, to prioritize impact over acceptance. The truth is, the people who hate you will never be satisfied. They'll find fault no matter what you do, twisting every decision into a moral failing. So why bother trying to appease them? If anything, their disdain is liberating. Once you stop caring about being liked, you can focus entirely on achieving your goals, without distraction, hesitation, or apology.

The Legacy of Hate

In the long run, hate often fades into admiration. Today's villains are tomorrow's visionaries. History has a way of forgiving ruthlessness when it comes with results. The industrialists who were once vilified as "robber barons" are now remembered as titans of industry. The tech moguls accused of monopolizing markets will likely be seen as the architects of a new era. Hate is temporary, but impact is permanent. So let them hate you. Wear it as a badge of honor, a sign that you're playing the game at a level they can't comprehend. Because if they hate you, it's not a sign you're doing something wrong, it's proof that you're doing it right.

Chapter 12
Preparing for the Revolution

Building Your Bunker- How to Stay Safe When the Peasants Revolt

No billionaire enjoys thinking about it, but the possibility of widespread unrest, a.k.a. the day the pitchforks come out, is a reality that can't be ignored. Wealth inequality, unchecked greed, and the increasingly precarious state of the planet have left society teetering on the edge. And while you might scoff at the idea of a full-scale revolt, every empire needs a contingency plan. A bunker isn't just a safeguard against disaster, it's an acknowledgment of your place in a fragile system that could collapse at any moment. Call it paranoia or call it preparation; either way, you'll be glad you thought ahead.

Step 1: Location, Location, Location

The first decision in building your bunker is where to put it. Forget urban centers—when the masses rise, the cities will be the first to descend into chaos. Instead, look for remote, defensible locations. Popular choices include secluded mountains, desert plains, or even hidden islands. New Zealand, in particular, has become a hot spot for billionaire bunkers, thanks to its isolation and relatively stable government.

Proximity to your primary residence is another factor to consider. While a far-flung retreat offers safety, it's useless if you can't reach it in time. If you live in a major city, consider building a secondary escape route into your bunker plans, a helipad or a private airstrip ensures you can make a swift getaway when things get dicey. For those willing to spend extravagantly (and let's be honest, you are), underground tunnels leading from your home to the bunker offer both convenience and discretion.

Step 2: Design for Survival and Style

A bunker isn't just a hole in the ground, it's your temporary kingdom. Functionality is important, but so is comfort. After all, what's the point of surviving the revolution if you're miserable while doing it? A well-designed bunker should be self-sustaining, luxurious, and intimidatingly high-tech.

At minimum, your bunker should include:
Reinforced Walls and Blast Doors: Built to withstand explosions, earthquakes, and unauthorized entry. Your fortress must be impenetrable to both natural disasters and disgruntled peasants.
Climate Control and Air Filtration: Essential for maintaining a livable environment, particularly if nuclear fallout or chemical attacks are part of your contingency planning.
Food and Water Supply: Stockpile non-perishable, gourmet-quality food. While the masses might fight over canned beans, you'll be dining on freeze-dried lobster bisque. Install advanced water purification systems and underground wells to ensure you never run dry.
Energy Independence: Solar panels, wind turbines, and geothermal systems are must-haves. Redundancy is key, one system might fail, but three won't.
Living Quarters: Bedrooms should rival those of a five-star resort, complete with king-sized beds, luxury linens, and en-suite bathrooms. A spacious living room, home theater, and game room will stave off boredom while you wait for the unrest to settle.
Command Center: A high-tech hub equipped with secure communications, surveillance feeds, and real-time data on the outside world. Staying informed is critical when planning your next move.

For added luxury, consider a gym, pool, and wine cellar. Remember, just because you're hiding doesn't mean you can't live well.

Step 3: Staff Your Sanctuary

A bunker without staff is just an elaborate cave. You'll need a carefully selected team to ensure your comfort and safety during your retreat. Key roles include:
Security Personnel: Ex-military or private contractors trained to protect you at all costs. Their job isn't just to keep intruders out, it's to remind anyone inside who's in charge.
Medical Professionals: A private doctor or nurse is essential for handling medical emergencies. Bonus points if they're also skilled in psychological counseling, you never know how long you'll be down there.
Chefs and Housekeepers: Even in the apocalypse, you deserve

gourmet meals and a spotless living environment.
Tech Specialists: Someone has to keep the power running, monitor communications, and fix any glitches in your surveillance systems.

Staffing your bunker also requires contingency planning. Pay them generously and treat them well to ensure their loyalty, after all, the last thing you want is an internal mutiny. And don't forget NDAs; even in a crisis, confidentiality is key.

Step 4: Security Measures

When the peasants revolt, your bunker must be a fortress. Advanced security measures are non-negotiable. Invest in:
Surveillance Systems: Cameras, motion sensors, and drones ensure you're always one step ahead of anyone approaching your sanctuary.
Automated Defenses: From electrified fences to autonomous drones, these systems discourage intruders without putting your security team at risk.
Biometric Access Controls: Fingerprint and retina scanners prevent unauthorized entry, ensuring only you and your trusted team can access the bunker.
Escape Routes: Even the best-designed bunkers can be breached. A hidden tunnel or secondary exit gives you a way out if the worst happens

Step 5: The Psychological Factor

Surviving in a bunker isn't just about physical safety, it's about maintaining morale. Isolation, uncertainty, and fear can take their toll, even on the most resilient billionaire. To keep spirits high:
Create a Routine: Structure your days with activities, meals, and exercise. Predictability brings a sense of control.
Entertainment Options: A well-stocked library, streaming services, and interactive games can distract from the chaos outside.
Social Connectivity: Even in isolation, communication with the outside world is crucial. Stay connected to trusted allies and advisors to remind yourself of your influence.

Step 6: Planning Your Return

The peasants' revolt won't last forever. When the time comes to emerge, you'll need a plan for reasserting your dominance. Your time in the bunker isn't just about survival, it's about strategizing for your comeback. Monitor the situation closely, using your command center to track political shifts, public sentiment, and economic opportunities.

When the dust settles, you won't just return, you'll seize the moment to solidify your power. Position yourself as the stabilizing force the world desperately needs, spinning your retreat as an act of wisdom rather than cowardice. Remind the masses that while they rioted, you were planning the future.

Embracing the Bunker Mentality

Building a bunker is more than just a precaution; it's a statement. It says that while others panic, you prepare. While they fight over scraps, you're dining in comfort. And while they rage against inequality, you're ensuring that no amount of upheaval can touch your empire.

Yes, it's cynical. Yes, it's dystopian. But in a world where your wealth and influence make you a target, a bunker isn't just about safety, it's about survival. And when the peasants revolt, survival is the only metric that matters.

gourmet meals and a spotless living environment.
Tech Specialists: Someone has to keep the power running, monitor communications, and fix any glitches in your surveillance systems.

Staffing your bunker also requires contingency planning. Pay them generously and treat them well to ensure their loyalty, after all, the last thing you want is an internal mutiny. And don't forget NDAs; even in a crisis, confidentiality is key.

Step 4: Security Measures

When the peasants revolt, your bunker must be a fortress. Advanced security measures are non-negotiable. Invest in:
Surveillance Systems: Cameras, motion sensors, and drones ensure you're always one step ahead of anyone approaching your sanctuary.
Automated Defenses: From electrified fences to autonomous drones, these systems discourage intruders without putting your security team at risk.
Biometric Access Controls: Fingerprint and retina scanners prevent unauthorized entry, ensuring only you and your trusted team can access the bunker.
Escape Routes: Even the best-designed bunkers can be breached. A hidden tunnel or secondary exit gives you a way out if the worst happens.

Step 5: The Psychological Factor

Surviving in a bunker isn't just about physical safety, it's about maintaining morale. Isolation, uncertainty, and fear can take their toll, even on the most resilient billionaire. To keep spirits high:
Create a Routine: Structure your days with activities, meals, and exercise. Predictability brings a sense of control.
Entertainment Options: A well-stocked library, streaming services, and interactive games can distract from the chaos outside.
Social Connectivity: Even in isolation, communication with the outside world is crucial. Stay connected to trusted allies and advisors to remind yourself of your influence.

Step 6: Planning Your Return

The peasants' revolt won't last forever. When the time comes to emerge, you'll need a plan for reasserting your dominance. Your time in the bunker isn't just about survival, it's about strategizing for your comeback. Monitor the situation closely, using your command center to track political shifts, public sentiment, and economic opportunities.

When the dust settles, you won't just return, you'll seize the moment to solidify your power. Position yourself as the stabilizing force the world desperately needs, spinning your retreat as an act of wisdom rather than cowardice. Remind the masses that while they rioted, you were planning the future.

Embracing the Bunker Mentality

Building a bunker is more than just a precaution; it's a statement. It says that while others panic, you prepare. While they fight over scraps, you're dining in comfort. And while they rage against inequality, you're ensuring that no amount of upheaval can touch your empire.

Yes, it's cynical. Yes, it's dystopian. But in a world where your wealth and influence make you a target, a bunker isn't just about safety, it's about survival. And when the peasants revolt, survival is the only metric that matters.

Private Armies and PR Wars- Protecting Your Wealth at All Costs

When you've amassed obscene wealth and influence, the world becomes a more dangerous place. Public resentment, political shifts, and growing inequality can all turn you into a target. To safeguard your empire, you need more than just legal teams and tax havens. You need two critical defenses: private armies and PR wars. Together, these tools protect your assets, your reputation, and, ultimately, your ability to maintain control.

Private Armies: The Hard Power of Wealth

Let's start with the blunt instrument: private security. At a certain level of wealth, hiring a bodyguard is quaint; you need a fully-fledged private army. These elite forces aren't just security guards, they're former special ops soldiers, intelligence operatives, and counter-terrorism experts. Their job is to ensure that no matter how volatile the world becomes, you remain untouchable.

A robust private security team includes armed personnel for physical protection, cybersecurity experts to prevent digital breaches, and surveillance specialists to keep an eye on potential threats. These forces operate discreetly, often blending into your surroundings or posing as innocuous staff, ensuring they don't detract from your public image. Their presence might seem excessive to the average person, but when your wealth is a magnet for danger, no precaution is too extreme.

Some billionaires even fund private militias to protect their physical assets, like vast estates or business operations in politically unstable regions. These forces aren't just about security, they're about projecting power. A private army signals that you're not just rich; you're untouchable. It reminds the world that while others are subject to the whims of governments and social movements, you're operating on your own terms.

PR Wars: Winning Hearts and Minds

While private armies protect your physical assets, PR wars protect something just as valuable: your reputation. A bad public image can lead to protests, boycotts, and even political action against you. To maintain your position, you need to control the narrative, spinning criticism into admiration and dissent into irrelevance.

The first step in winning a PR war is monitoring public sentiment. Social media listening tools, hired PR firms, and even private intelligence teams can track how people perceive you in real time. This data allows you to preemptively address criticism, ensuring that the story being told about you is the one you want people to hear.

Once you know what people are saying, the real work begins: reframing the narrative. Are you being criticized for exploiting workers? Launch a campaign highlighting your "commitment to job creation." Facing backlash over environmental practices? Announce a new green initiative (whether or not it amounts to meaningful change). The key is to present yourself as a visionary leader whose actions, however controversial, are always in service of a greater good.

Social media is a battlefield in PR wars, and you'll need an army of your own here, too—albeit a digital one. Bots, influencers, and carefully curated ad campaigns can flood platforms with positive messages about you and your work. Critics will call it propaganda, but it's really just smart branding. The louder your message, the harder it becomes for dissenting voices to cut through the noise.

The Intersection of Armies and PR

The true genius of combining private armies and PR wars lies in their intersection. One protects your wealth in the physical realm, while the other ensures that your power remains intact in the ideological one. For example, when a security incident occurs, say, a protest outside your headquarters—your PR team can frame the response as a necessary measure to ensure public safety, painting you as the responsible party.

These tactics also work in tandem during crises. A data breach or scandal can be swiftly addressed by your PR team, while your private security forces ensure that whistleblowers or leaks don't escalate further. The goal is to create a seamless defense, where every potential threat, whether physical, digital, or reputational, is neutralized before it can cause significant harm.

The Moral Cost of Paranoia

Of course, building private armies and waging PR wars comes with its own costs, financial, social, and ethical. There's an undeniable dystopian undertone to hiring militias and flooding social media with propaganda, but when your wealth is on the line, morality often takes a back seat to pragmatism. The reality is that the world you've helped create, a world of inequality and unrest, necessitates these defenses. And while you might occasionally feel a twinge of guilt, it's nothing compared to the fear of losing everything.

Some will call you paranoid; others will call you prepared. The truth lies somewhere in between. These strategies aren't just about safeguarding wealth, they're about safeguarding the systems that allow wealth like yours to exist. Your private armies and PR wars aren't just protecting you; they're protecting the status quo.

The Endgame

Ultimately, private armies and PR wars are tools of survival in a world that increasingly questions the concentration of power and wealth. They ensure that no matter how much the masses resent you or how hard activists push for change, your empire remains unshaken. Because at the end of the day, protecting your wealth isn't just about what you've built, it's about who you are. And you didn't get this far by letting anyone take that away.

Controlling the Narrative in Chaos- Staying the hero even when the world turns

Controlling the narrative in chaos is not just a skill; it is an art, a calculated dance that ensures you remain the hero even when the world seems determined to cast you as the villain. Chaos, whether it manifests as economic downturns, environmental crises, or public outcry against inequality, is a threat to the fragile ecosystem of wealth and power you've built. Yet, chaos is also an opportunity, a malleable moment when the loudest voice and the most compelling story define reality. In such moments, staying the hero is not about avoiding blame or sidestepping scrutiny, it's about owning the story, reshaping the perception of events so thoroughly that even those who suffer under your decisions believe in your nobility. When the world turns against you, your first move is to embrace the chaos as evidence of your indispensability. Frame the instability not as a consequence of your actions but as the natural turbulence of a world in flux, a world that needs leaders like you to restore balance. Lean into the rhetoric of inevitability: you didn't create the crisis, but you are uniquely positioned to fix it. Whether you're laying off thousands in the name of "streamlining operations" or lobbying against regulations under the guise of "protecting innovation," every action must be cast as a sacrifice on your part for the greater good. Let them see you as the reluctant warrior, forced into difficult decisions by forces beyond your control but always acting with the future in mind.

The tools to shape this narrative are as varied as the chaos itself. Media appearances, social media posts, carefully staged photo opportunities, each becomes a brushstroke in the masterpiece of your public persona. When you speak, your tone must convey both authority and empathy, a delicate balance that assures people you're in charge without alienating them with your wealth or power. If layoffs or controversies arise, your response should be a symphony of regret and resolve, painting you as someone who "understands the pain" but must act for the "survival of the many." Use language that invokes progress, resilience, and a shared journey. You are not a billionaire operating in isolation; you are a steward of collective hopes and dreams, or at least that's how the story should feel. Even when your actions exacerbate the chaos, ensure the public perceives you as working tirelessly to contain it, to guide society through the storm.

Chaos thrives on visibility, and so should you. When the world turns, people crave a figurehead to blame or a hero to follow. By stepping into the spotlight strategically, you can ensure that blame shifts elsewhere while your heroism shines. In times of environmental crises, announce investments in green initiatives, regardless of their actual impact. During economic upheavals, pledge to support small businesses, even if the terms favor your empire more than theirs. When protests erupt against inequality, convene panels and discussions to "listen" and "understand," presenting yourself as a bridge-builder even if you have no intention of altering the structures that caused the anger. Perception becomes reality when repeated often enough, and in chaos, repetition is your ally. The more people see you addressing issues, the less they'll question whether you're part of the problem.

Critics will inevitably try to poke holes in your narrative, but chaos weakens their platform as much as it strengthens yours. People are too distracted, too overwhelmed to dig deep into nuance. Use this to your advantage. Respond to criticism with calm deflections that emphasize your dedication to solutions over squabbles. If questioned about uncomfortable truths, say, your wealth increasing during a global recession, point instead to the jobs your empire provides or the philanthropic gestures you've made. Never let the conversation linger on accountability; redirect it to your vision of the future. Chaos, for all its destruction, is fertile ground for reinvention. Every criticism becomes an opportunity to double down on your story, every accusation a chance to contrast your supposed composure with the disorder around you.

Ultimately, controlling the narrative in chaos isn't just about staying the hero, it's about becoming indispensable. The world should see your actions, however self-serving, as integral to its survival. You don't just run a business; you stabilize industries. You don't just make decisions; you shape futures. In the fog of chaos, you aren't merely a participant; you're the lighthouse guiding everyone else to safety. Whether history will judge you kindly is a question for another day, and honestly, one that matters far less than ensuring that today's story leaves you standing tall. By the time the dust settles, the world will remember the chaos, but only through the lens you've created. If you've done it right, they won't just see you as a hero, they'll believe they couldn't have made it through without you.

Planning Your Exit Strategy- Escaping to safe havens

When the walls start closing in and the golden age of unchecked wealth begins to crack under the weight of public outrage, political reform, or economic collapse, every billionaire needs an exit strategy. The ability to retreat to a safe haven isn't just about survival, it's about preserving the lifestyle, assets, and influence that define you. Planning your exit strategy is less about running away and more about staying ahead, ensuring you remain untouchable as the rest of the world catches fire. The process isn't for the faint of heart, requiring meticulous foresight, unflinching pragmatism, and a willingness to abandon ship at just the right moment.

The first step in crafting an effective exit strategy is identifying your safe haven. The ideal location must combine political stability, favorable tax laws, and a discreet respect for wealth. Traditional choices like Switzerland, Singapore, or the Cayman Islands remain top contenders for their combination of financial secrecy and security. For those seeking physical and geopolitical isolation, New Zealand's remote countryside or a private Caribbean island offers an added layer of safety. The location must also align with your broader goals: do you want to blend into an exclusive community of fellow elites, or do you prefer isolation where no one can reach you? Every detail matters, from the availability of private airstrips to the proximity of luxury amenities that ensure your exile feels more like an extended vacation than a retreat.

Once you've chosen your destination, the next step is securing the infrastructure to support your new life. A private compound or estate isn't just a home, it's a fortress. Your property must be equipped with top-tier security systems, renewable energy sources, and enough resources to sustain you and your family indefinitely. Think bunkers, helipads, and private docks. Food supplies, water purification systems, and advanced medical facilities are non-negotiable, as is the staff to maintain them. Security personnel, chefs, personal assistants, and even teachers for your children can ensure that your standard of living remains uncompromised, even as the world outside your gates descends into chaos.

But the escape plan doesn't end with logistics; it also requires financial finesse. Moving your assets into trusts, offshore accounts, or cryptocurrencies minimizes exposure and keeps your wealth untouchable. Start the process discreetly, transferring funds and reassigning ownership long before any potential upheaval. While the masses may call it hoarding or tax evasion, you understand it as prudence, ensuring that the fortune you've built remains intact regardless of what laws or movements arise in your home country. Diversify holdings across jurisdictions to prevent governments or activists from targeting your empire in one fell swoop. If the worst comes to pass, your wealth should be as mobile as you are.

Equally important is maintaining the façade of normalcy for as long as possible. Publicly, you should continue to act as though you're fully invested in the community, the nation, or the cause. Make speeches, attend galas, and issue press releases expressing your "commitment to shared prosperity" even as your jets are quietly fueled and ready for departure. The illusion of stability buys you time and keeps your adversaries guessing. When the moment to leave arrives, it should be swift, seamless, and as invisible as possible.

A critical part of your exit strategy is managing your narrative post-departure. Once you've escaped, the story cannot be one of abandonment, it must be framed as a noble step back. You're not fleeing public accountability or the collapse of systems you helped create; you're "reassessing priorities" or "exploring opportunities to expand your global perspective." Use philanthropy as a shield, funding causes that generate goodwill and redirect attention away from your retreat. If criticism arises, dismiss it as shortsightedness from those who don't understand the complexities of leadership or the sacrifices required to maintain stability.

Despite its meticulous planning, an exit strategy is not without its emotional toll. There is an undeniable emptiness in leaving behind the empire you built, even if it's temporary. But the calculus is simple: better to live lavishly in exile than risk losing everything to forces beyond your control. The reality is that a safe haven isn't just a retreat, it's a reminder that you operate on a different plane, one where survival isn't dictated by governments, economies, or public opinion but by your ability to remain one step ahead. An exit strategy isn't a failure; it's a masterstroke, proof that even as the world burns, you hold the reins of your destiny.

Epilogue
Greed is an Illness, You Are Ill

Embracing the Billionaire Lifestyle While the World Crumbles

There's a sickness at the heart of the billionaire lifestyle, an affliction so pervasive it's mistaken for ambition, innovation, or brilliance. But let's call it what it is: greed. Not the simple desire for more, but a pathological, unquenchable hunger that consumes everything in its path, including the people who wield it. Greed is an illness, and you, billionaire, are deeply unwell. The symptoms are all there, the compulsive accumulation of wealth, the obsessive need for control, and the staggering blindness to the harm you cause. While the world crumbles under the weight of inequality, environmental collapse, and social unrest, you sit atop your empire of excess, clutching tighter to the riches that have already rotted your soul.

Greed, like any disease, has its justifications. You tell yourself that your wealth is a reflection of your talent and hard work, that the system rewarded you fairly for the value you created. But deep down, even you don't believe that. You know how the game is played, how the rules are written by people like you to ensure that wealth flows upward and stays there. Your billions aren't the result of ingenuity alone, they're the spoils of a system designed to extract more from the many to enrich the few. And yet, instead of questioning this system, you embrace it, perpetuate it, expand it. Why? Because greed doesn't know when to stop. It's not satisfied with enough; it demands everything.

This illness distorts your reality, twisting your perception of the world and your place in it. You see the rising inequality, the collapsing ecosystems, the anger bubbling beneath the surface, but you convince yourself that none of it is your fault. How could it be, when you're doing so much "good"? Haven't you donated to charities, started foundations, and funded research to save the planet? You lean on these acts of philanthropy as if they're a cure for the disease that drives you, but they're not. They're symptoms, gestures designed to alleviate your guilt while ensuring nothing truly changes. You might think of yourself as a savior, but you're more like a parasite—feeding off the world while offering just enough back to keep it from expelling you.

What makes greed so insidious is its ability to mask itself as progress. You don't see your yachts, private jets, and sprawling estates as excess; you see them as the rewards of hard work and vision. You don't see your monopolies or tax havens as exploitation; you see them as strategic genius. And when the world pushes back, when protests erupt or governments threaten reform, you don't see it as a reckoning, you see it as an attack. This is the ultimate delusion of greed: the belief that you are not only entitled to more than anyone else but that this entitlement is somehow righteous.

But even as you clutch at your riches, even as you retreat to your private islands and fortified estates, you cannot escape the emptiness gnawing at you. Greed is a bottomless pit, and no amount of wealth can fill it. Every new acquisition, a bigger yacht, a rarer piece of art, another billion dollars, isn't a solution; it's a distraction, a desperate attempt to ignore the void. You tell yourself that your lifestyle is proof of your success, but what is it really? A fortress built to shield you from a world that you've helped to ruin, a gilded cage that keeps you trapped in your own sickness.

The irony, of course, is that even as you distance yourself from the chaos, you are inextricably tied to it. Your wealth depends on the very systems that are collapsing under the weight of inequality and exploitation. The labor of workers, the stability of governments, the health of ecosystems, these are the foundations of your empire, and they are crumbling. And yet, instead of using your influence to address these crises, you double down on the lifestyle that exacerbates them. Greed blinds you to the inevitability of collapse, convincing you that your wealth can insulate you from consequences. But it can't. The walls of your compound may be high, but they are not impenetrable. The jets may be fast, but they cannot outrun the reckoning.

And let's not pretend you're unaware of your illness. Deep down, in the moments when the noise fades and the emptiness becomes impossible to ignore, you feel it. You know that your greed has consumed you, that it has made you complicit in a world spiraling toward disaster. You know that your philanthropy is a bandage on a wound that demands amputation, that your lifestyle is unsustainable, and that the fortress you've built around yourself is not a sanctuary but a prison. But to confront these truths would mean admitting your illness, and greed does not allow for self-reflection. It demands justification, rationalization, denial.

So you carry on, embracing the billionaire lifestyle as the world crumbles around you. You host galas to discuss sustainability while flying in on carbon-spewing jets. You fund panels on inequality while your companies fight against fair wages and unionization. You lament the state of the planet while sipping champagne in your climate-controlled mansion. These contradictions are not anomalies, they are the essence of your existence. Greed doesn't just tolerate hypocrisy; it thrives on it.

The most tragic part of all this is that greed has robbed you of what truly matters. The wealth you hoard cannot buy connection, meaning, or peace. Your vast empire, built on exploitation and excess, isolates you from the world and from yourself. And as the planet burns, as inequality deepens and anger rises, you will find that your wealth is not a shield but a target, a symbol of everything that is broken. The reckoning will come, and when it does, your yachts, jets, and compounds will not save you. They will only serve as monuments to your sickness, reminders of a life spent taking far more than you ever gave.

In the end, greed is not just your illness, it is your legacy. And as the world collapses under the weight of everything you've built, it will not remember you as a visionary or a hero. It will remember you as a symptom of a system that failed, a cautionary tale of what happens when greed is left unchecked. You may not care now, but you will. Because greed, for all its power, cannot protect you from the truth: that you, billionaire, are sick, and the world is paying the price for your illness.

Appendices- Must-Have Yachts and Jets for the Discerning Billionaire

When you've reached the apex of wealth, your possessions aren't just luxuries, they're statements of power. Few symbols of success convey your status as effectively as yachts and private jets. These aren't merely modes of transportation; they're floating and flying palaces that scream exclusivity, indulgence, and untouchable influence. Below is your essential guide to must-have yachts and jets for the billionaire lifestyle.

Yachts

M/Y Azzam – *$600 million*
At over 590 feet long, this superyacht is one of the largest in the world. With sleek, modern interiors and speeds of over 30 knots, it combines luxury and performance like no other. A yacht fit for hosting world leaders, or simply lounging in unparalleled comfort.
Eclipse – *$500 million*
Owned by Roman Abramovich, this yacht boasts two helipads, a submarine, and an anti-paparazzi laser system. Perfect for billionaires who value privacy as much as extravagance.
Solaris – *$600 million*
A cutting-edge superyacht with an emphasis on sustainability. Its hybrid propulsion system allows for eco-friendly cruising—because nothing says "environmentally conscious" like a $600 million yacht.

Jets

Gulfstream G700 – *$75 million*
With its spacious cabins, cutting-edge technology, and transcontinental range, the G700 is the gold standard for business aviation. A flying office and luxury suite rolled into one.
Bombardier Global 7500 – *$75 million*
Known for its smooth ride and luxurious interior, this jet offers a range of over 7,700 nautical miles, ensuring you can jet-set without limits.
Boeing Business Jet 747-8 – *$400 million*
For the billionaire who thinks a regular private jet just won't do, the BBJ 747-8 transforms a commercial airliner into a flying palace with bespoke interiors, bedrooms, and conference rooms.

Suggested Therapists for Billionaires (Because You Have Feelings Too)

Even billionaires need someone to talk to, someone who won't judge you for lamenting the complexities of private jet maintenance or the existential burden of owning too many homes. The weight of unimaginable wealth can be isolating, and let's face it, your friends (or yes-people) aren't going to call you out when you spiral into self-pity. That's where therapists come in: impartial, nonjudgmental, and trained to handle even the most rarefied existential crises. Here's a list of the types of therapists perfectly suited to meet your unique needs.

High-Net-Worth Mental Health Specialists

These therapists specialize in the psychological challenges faced by the ultra-wealthy. They understand that your problems are "different" and won't roll their eyes when you mention how exhausting it is to choose between two Caribbean islands for your winter retreat.
- Recommended: Dr. Timothy Should Find Another Job, known for his work with CEOs and celebrities, offers discreet, personalized sessions tailored to navigating power, isolation, and legacy anxiety.

Existential Wealth Counselors

For billionaires grappling with the meaning of it all, existential wealth therapists dive deep into questions about purpose and fulfillment. If philanthropy feels hollow and another yacht doesn't spark joy, they're here to help.
- Recommended: Dr. Emily Empathy Lacking, author of *"If Only I Had a Heart and Weren't Destroying the Planet"*

Stress and Image Management Experts

If the public's disdain is eating at you, these therapists can help you reconcile your feelings with your reality—or at least teach you how to sleep through the backlash.
- Recommended: Dr. Vanessa Really Bad at Humanity, specializes in helping billionaires handle media scrutiny, societal judgment, and "rich guilt."

A Wealth Checklist- Do You Matter Yet?

Being wealthy isn't just about the money, it's about making sure the world knows you're *important*. This handy checklist will help you determine whether you've crossed the threshold into billionaire significance, or if you're still just a very rich nobody.

Assets That Scream "I've Arrived"

Do you own at least one private island?
Is your home so large that you've gotten lost in it (more than once)?
Does your art collection include at least one piece you had to "pry" from a museum's clutches?

Vehicles That Double as Status Symbols

Do you own both a superyacht *and* a backup yacht (for the staff, of course)?
Is your private jet customized with a bedroom, a conference room, and a personal chef on standby?
Does your car collection include at least one hypercar valued higher than most people's lifetime earnings?

Power and Influence

Have you personally lobbied a politician, or, funded their campaign?
Is your phone full of direct contacts for CEOs, world leaders, and at least one royal family?
Have you bought controlling interest in a company, not because it's profitable, but because you didn't like the way they talked about you?

Vanity Metrics

Is a building, foundation, or stadium named after you (preferably one you funded with *just* enough to get your name on it)?
Do you have a memoir in progress, detailing your "humble start"?
Has anyone created a social media hate thread or conspiracy theory centered around your wealth?

If you've checked most of these boxes, congratulations: you're officially rich enough to matter. If not, better hustle, your private island isn't going to buy itself.

List of Prints

1. Billionaire Uno — 8
2. Chicken, It's What's for Dinner — 14
3. More, More, More — 32
4. Yatzi! — 42
5. Yachtzi! — 50
6. Island of One, I Have no Soul — 58
7. Do as I say, Not as I do — 66
8. Off With Their Head — 78
9. Walk Amongst the People — 94
10. Cholera in the Time of Love — 112
11. Bigger is Not Always Better — 124
12. Puppet Monster, You Are, Not Us — 136
13. Build the Wall, At Last — 150
14. Asylum Is Not Just for Immigrants — 162
15. Me Never Thee — 166

About the author

The author lives removed.

Please feel free to burn part or all of this book, safely, as an effigy.

www.ingramcontent.com/pod-product-compliance
Lightning Source LLC
Chambersburg PA
CBHW020933090426
42736CB00010B/1125